The Revolutiona[...]
Everyone's T[...]

THE
LET
THEM
PRINCIPLE

Inspired by Mel Robbins' Teaching

MELISSA GREEN

Contents

INTRODUCTION: THE POWER OF TWO SIMPLE WORDS i

The Origins of The Let Them Principle...i

Why This Book Matters...iv

How To Use This Book...iv

CHAPTER 1: UNDERSTANDING THE LET THEM PRINCIPLE
..1

What Does "Let Them" Really Mean? 1

The Science Behind Letting Go.. 4

Why Control Creates Stress.. 6

CHAPTER 2: REDEFINING RELATIONSHIPS 10

Identifying Draining Relationships................................... 10

Let Them Be: Building Boundaries With Ease............................ 17

How To Recognize And Nurturehealt Hy Connections 23

CHAPTER 3: MASTERING EMOTIONAL FREEDOM 29

Breaking Free From People's Opinions.................................29

Handling Criticism Without Losing Confidence 35

Finding Joy In Letting Go... 40

CHAPTER 4: BUILDING UNSHAKABLE CONFIDENCE 46

The Connection Between Control And Self-Doubt 46

Letting Go Of Perfectionism... 49

Embracing Authenticity 54

CHAPTER 5: CULTIVATING RESILIENCE & PEACE 61

Techniques To Stop Wasting Energy On Others 61

Shifting Focus To What Truly Matters 65

Creating A Calm And Centered Mindset 70

CHAPTER 6: PRACTICAL APPLICATIONS OF THE LET THEM PRINCIPLE **74**

At Work: Navigating Toxicity And Managing Expectations 74

In Love: Strengthening Romantic Relationships 79

With Family And Friends: Letting Go Of Unrealistic Demands 87

CHAPTER 7: DESIGNING A LIFE YOU LOVE **95**

Prioritizing Your Goals Over External Noise 95

Daily Practices To Stay In Control Of Your Energy 101

Living With Intention And Joy 105

CONCLUSION: EMBRACING ENDLESS POSSIBILITIES **112**

The Long-Term Benefits Of Letting Them... 112

Your Journey To Lasting Peace And Confidence....................................... 116

The Power of Two
Simple Words

THE ORIGINS OF THE LET THEM PRINCIPLE

T he A sophisticated conceptual framework known as "Let Them Principle" reframes how people view relationships and outside influences in their lives. Two words sum up its simplicity: Let Them. Fundamentally, this idea creates room for serenity, independence, and confidence by reorienting the attention from controlling others to accepting what is out of one's control. It is about cultivating an attitude that puts one's health ahead of pointless conflicts, not about being passive or indifferent. Mel Robbins popularized this concept, which has struck a deep chord with people who are looking for ways to cope with stress, irritation, and self-doubt.

The Let Them Principle has its origins in the human inclination to make significant financial investments in controlling, swaying, or appeasing other people. People are frequently conditioned by society to feel that their worth is found in their capacity to control events, improve circumstances, or live up to expectations. A vicious cycle of stress and dissatisfaction is produced by this ongoing pressure to succeed, particularly when results are beyond one's control. Robbins noted that a lot of individuals expend a lot of energy worrying about the actions, viewpoints, or decisions of others, which results in emotional weariness. An intentional choice to cease controlling others and instead concentrate on one's own development and tranquility gave rise to the Let Them Principle.

The idea is based on a combination of behavioral and psychological concepts. Humans have a natural desire for control, as psychological research has long demonstrated, but this urge frequently backfires when it spreads to areas outside of their control. In addition to making people angry, trying to control them can damage relationships and undermine one's self-esteem. This theory is also supported by neuroscience, which shows that the brain functions best when it is focused on an internal locus of control—situations in which one has agency—instead of external stressors. By encouraging people to focus inward, the Let Them Principle helps people avoid needless stress and promote emotional balance.

The theory's applicability is one of its main features. It challenges people to stand back and consider what is most important in their lives. For example, the Let Them Principle recommends posing the potent query, "What happens if I simply let them?" when someone acts in a way that feels cruel or falls short of expectations. This method acknowledges that some behaviors or attitudes are beyond one's control, but it does not imply endorsing destructive behavior. People can save energy for things that are consistent with their priorities and values by letting go of the impulse to correct, persuade, or retaliate.

Additionally, the approach is consistent with ageless ideologies like mindfulness exercises and stoicism. The Let Them Principle echoes the stoic philosophy of accepting what is beyond one's control and concentrating on what is under one's control. In a similar vein, mindfulness teaches people how to observe without passing judgment, which enables them to distance themselves from emotional triggers. Robbins incorporates these ideas within a contemporary, approachable framework that appeals to audiences today.

The Let Them Principle's immediate, relatable impact is partly responsible for its success. When a buddy cancels plans, a coworker takes credit for their ideas, or a family member gives unsolicited advice, people frequently become frustrated. Anger, bitterness, or an effort to make things right could be the natural response. A different approach is recommended by the Let Them Principle: accept the circumstances, let the individual alone, and concentrate on the things that are under your control. When people realize they no longer have to bear the emotional weight of other people's decisions, this small change frequently results in an unanticipated sense of relief.

The theory's appeal also resides in its ability to improve relationships. Unfulfilled expectations or attempts to influence others are the root cause of many disputes. People can create healthier relationships based on acceptance and respect for one another by letting go of the impulse to control. Allowing them does not imply lowering standards or permitting destructive behavior to continue, Robbins stresses. Rather, it entails establishing boundaries between acceptance and influence so that genuine connections can thrive. Those who suffer from people-pleasing, perfectionism, or fear of being judged will find the Let Them Principle particularly transformative. These characteristics frequently cause people to overextend themselves in an effort to satisfy everyone's demands at the price of their own well-being. It offers a freeing alternative: instead of trying to please everyone, let people believe what they want, feel what they feel, and do what they would want. People are empowered to live confidently and genuinely as a result of this change, which lessens the burden of external validation.

The Let Them Principle's emphasis on introspection is another important feature. People are urged to evaluate their own motivations and responses when using the theory. Why am I offended by someone's actions? Is it worth my energy to deal with this? But what if I left them alone? By asking these questions, people can stop the cycle of emotional response and acquire perspective and clarity. Developing the inner serenity and self-assurance that the Let Them Principle promises requires this introspective approach, which is not always simple.

The principle is simple, but it takes intention and practice to put into effect. It might be difficult to resist the impulse to dispute, fix, or intervene when emotions are running high. Robbins advises beginning small—picking one relationship or situation to apply the theory to and seeing what happens. This technique reduces emotional triggers and rewires thought patterns over time, eventually becoming a habit.

The Let Them Principle's goals go beyond lowering stress. It's about taking back control of one's life. People make space for their own growth and self-discovery by letting others be. They can direct their energies toward endeavors that complement their values, aspirations, and passions. This change not only increases personal fulfillment but also boosts confidence since people understand they can succeed without having to control outside factors. Because it tackles a universal pain point—the conflict between the desire to affect others and the reality of limited control—the Let Them Principle strikes a deep chord with individuals. It provides a straightforward, doable remedy that satisfies the fundamental human need for liberty and harmony. People can escape the draining cycle of overanalyzing, overreacting, and overextending themselves by embracing this way of thinking. They might instead choose to live a life that is clear, purposeful, and self-assured, based on the knowledge that real power comes from mastering oneself rather than from dominating others.

The Let Them Principle is essentially a way of life rather than just a tool. It encourages people to put their mental and emotional well-being first by challenging deeply rooted behaviors and social standards. A life full of serenity, freedom, and unwavering confidence can be created by people by letting go of pointless conflicts and concentrating on what really matters. Millions are still motivated by the Let Them Principle's simplicity and applicability, which demonstrates that even the tiniest changes in viewpoint can lead to significant change.

WHY THIS BOOK MATTERS

The Let Them Principle is more than simply a catchphrase; it's a profound shift in perspective that has the power to change people's lives. This book is important because it offers useful advice and doable methods for understanding the idea in order to attain personal freedom, self-assurance, and serenity. Letting up on needless control is not only beneficial but crucial in a society full of social pressures, interpersonal conflicts, and internal conflicts.

The understanding that a large portion of life's stress stems from attempting to control circumstances that are really beyond our control is at the core of this idea. This constant desire, whether it is to alter the thoughts, behaviors, or emotions of others, frequently leaves people exhausted and frustrated. By learning the power of Let Them, people can recover the energy they expend on these pointless endeavors and refocus it on worthwhile endeavors. This change is about setting better boundaries that put one's own well-being first, not about disengaging from relationships or life.

This book's emphasis on peace is among the factors that make it so important. Many people suffer from anxiety, tension, or a feeling of overwhelm, which frequently results from their social interactions. These moments can feel overwhelming, whether it's the annoyance of a friend abruptly canceling plans, the disappointment of a coworker's criticism, or the hurt of a family member's hurtful remarks. According to the Let Them Principle, we don't have to let these circumstances control how we feel. We may greatly lessen the mental and emotional toll of such exchanges by letting people act as they will and concentrating on the things we can control, such as our responses, choices, and priorities.

Consider a parent who is always under stress because their adult child isn't making decisions in life that they agree with. In an effort to "fix" the situation, this parent may argue, give unsolicited advice, or worry for hours. A different strategy is recommended by the Let Them Principle, which emphasizes preserving a caring, supporting relationship while acknowledging that the child has their own path. The parent can maintain harmony while providing unwavering support by allowing the youngster to make their own decisions. Another important area where this book has transformative potential is confidence. A lot of people base their feeling of value on what other people think of them. They frequently sacrifice their authenticity in an effort to be liked, accepted, or validated. This produces a brittle sense of self that is readily broken by rejection or criticism. By educating people to quit seeking approval from others, Mastering the Power of Let Them breaks this cycle. Rather, it motivates individuals to concentrate on their innate principles and objectives. This change enables people to develop a solid, unwavering confidence that is independent of other people's perceptions.

Consider a person who is hesitant to pursue their ideal career because they are afraid their family won't approve. They can understand that, although their family's ideas are legitimate, it is not their job to control them by using the Let Them Principle. The person may concentrate on what is really important to them—creating a career they love—by letting their family think as they choose. This increased self-assurance not only gives individuals the courage to take risks but also cultivates a greater sense of fulfillment and self-worth.

Perhaps the most liberating feature of the Let Them Principle is the freedom it offers. Social expectations, cultural conventions, or even individual people-pleasing behaviors may make a lot of things in life feel like responsibilities. Because they are always changing their conduct to avoid conflict or disappointment, these invisible ties prevent people from leading real lives. By highlighting the fact that we are not in charge of controlling the emotions or expectations of others, this book destroys those bonds. Allowing others to do, speak, or think as they like makes room for people to live their lives as they see fit.

Imagine a situation when someone is chastised for a lifestyle decision, such as choosing to be childless or unmarried. In the absence of the Let Them Principle, they might use effort defending their choice, feeling bad about it, or even altering their decisions to please other people. When they grasp the notion, they realize that other people's opinions are theirs to maintain, not theirs to alter. They are able to make decisions that are consistent with their values and desires and proceed without apology as a result of this knowledge.

The fact that this book connects theory and practice makes it significant as well. Even though the idea of "letting go" is not new, many individuals find it difficult to put it into practice in everyday situations. Intellectually knowing that other people's actions shouldn't impact you is one thing, but acting on that knowledge when emotions are running high is quite another. In order to help you understand the Let Them Principle and apply it successfully in your everyday life, this book offers step-by-step instructions, realistic examples, and useful activities. The methods provided here are intended to make the theory a lived experience, whether that means learning to set boundaries with grace, rephrasing circumstances to lessen emotional triggers, or pausing before reacting.

Furthermore, the Let Them Principle affects more than just the individual. The adoption of this perspective by one partner in a relationship frequently encourages others to follow suit. The relationship may become more cooperative and harmonious, for instance, if a spouse quits attempting to micromanage their partner's behaviors. When a friend allows others to vent without attempting to resolve their issues, they may observe that their relationships grow less tense and more sincere. People can support the development of a mutually respectful and understanding culture by setting an example of this approach.

More broadly, this book tackles a basic reality of life: we can't control everything, and that's okay. Letting go of things that don't benefit us is the key to mastering the power of Let Them, not giving up. It all comes down to deciding to invest our limited energy wisely. This viewpoint is particularly helpful in the fast-paced, highly linked world of today, where it's simple to feel like you're being tugged in a hundred different directions. People can focus on what is really important to them and cut through the clutter by adopting the Let Them Principle.

In the end, this book is important because it gives people the tools they need to regain their freedom, peace, and self-assurance in a straightforward and useful manner. It's about practical actions that anyone can take to better their life, not about grandiose ideas or abstract ideologies. You can learn to let go of things that are beyond their control, maintain your integrity, and design a truly fulfilling life by mastering the power of let them. Even while this path is not always simple, it is always worthwhile, and the rewards go much beyond the person to their relationships, communities, and sense of purpose in life.

HOW TO USE THIS BOOK

The purpose of this book is to serve as your helpful guide as you work to master the power of let them. The best way to use it is as a toolkit for making major changes in your life and mindset, not just a list of ideas. This manual will show you how to interact with the content in a way that gives you the ability to develop freedom, self-assurance, and serenity. Approaching the text with an open mind is the first step. Some long-held ideas about how to engage with people and handle relationships may be called into question by the ideas in the Let Them Principle. Instead of reading each chapter quickly, take your time. As you go along, think about how the ideas relate to your own experiences. The book's scenarios and examples are intended to be relatable to actual events, providing you with a framework to view your current situation from a different angle.

To lay a strong foundation, begin with the introduction. This part lays the groundwork for comprehending the remainder of the book and explains why the Let Them Principle is revolutionary. Proceed to the main chapters after that, paying close attention to each one as a separate building block. Despite their connections, each chapter focuses on a different facet of putting the theory into practice. Treat each chapter as an in-depth exploration of practical tactics, whether the focus is on developing confidence, establishing boundaries, or learning to relinquish control.

Make notes while you read in order to properly interact with the content. note the main ideas, activities, and techniques that most appeal to you. There is a lot of useful advice in this book, and it will be simpler to go back and use the ideas in your everyday life if you keep a personal journal of what stands out. To improve your comprehension of the ideas, consider the questions and prompts at the conclusion of each chapter. These activities aid in lesson internalization and cognitive integration.

Treating this book as a living resource is one of the best ways to use it. Instead of finishing it all at once, take some time to apply the teachings in real-world situations in between chapters. For instance, if a chapter emphasizes letting go of other people's perspectives, practice this way of thinking in your relationships for a few days. See how it impacts your relationships, choices, and feelings. As it allows you to quantify the observable changes in your life, journaling can be a useful tool in this process.

Additionally, this book promotes introspection. As you read, consider your most stressful, annoying, or powerless situations. Reframe these difficulties using the Let Them Principle and consider how you can gain from taking a more laid-back, accepting stance. For example, if a coworker's behavior regularly irritates you, think about how allowing them to act as they like while keeping your attention on your own behavior may reduce your annoyance and increase your output.

The book also offers useful exercises that are intended to assist you in incorporating its lessons. Give these workouts your full attention. These activities serve as a link between theory and practice, whether you're practicing detachment, establishing boundaries, or clarifying your own ideals. Consider them experimental, and be prepared to modify them to suit your particular situation. Recall that progress toward a life of more freedom and peace, not perfection, is the aim.

Another effective method to utilize the ideas in this book is to share them with others. You can gain fresh insights and a deeper understanding of the Let Them Principle by talking about it with loved ones, friends, or a mentor you can trust. Share your experiences with the concepts you've learned, explain them, and encourage others to learn more about the idea. This not only helps you learn more, but it also gives you and your relationships the chance to grow together. Rereading this book over time is also crucial. Gaining mastery of the Let Them Principle is a continuous process rather than a one-time event. As your situation evolves and you face new obstacles, the teachings in this book will still be applicable. Keep it handy as a reference manual, and don't be afraid to go back and review any chapters or exercises that seem especially pertinent to your current circumstances. Depending on your journey, each reread may reveal new insights.

Finally, use the book's conclusion as a chance to summarize what you've learned. Think back on the main ideas and their effect on your attitude and actions. This section should be used to make plans for future applications of the Let Them Principle. By the time you're done, you'll know exactly how to live a more tranquil, self-assured, and independent life and will have the resources to maintain these improvements over time.

This book is not a prescription; it is a guide. By concentrating on the things you can control and letting go of the things you cannot, it is intended to give you the confidence to take charge of your life. You may fully realize its ability to change your perspective and build an authentic, fulfilling life by engaging it with intention, introspection, and a dedication to applying its lessons.

CHAPTER 1

Understanding the Let Them Principle

WHAT DOES "LET THEM" REALLY MEAN?

The core idea behind the phrase "Let Them" lies in the intentional release of control over other people's actions, choices, and behaviors. This idea represents a significant departure from the ingrained urge to control, sway, or forecast the choices of others. It encourages you to concentrate on the things you can control, such as your responses, decisions, and attitude, rather than wasting your time trying to change other people or circumstances. Fundamentally, the "Let Them" mentality teaches you to disengage from the pointless burdens that frequently impede relationships and interactions, paving the way for emotional and mental freedom.

"Let Them" does not imply that you accept or condone someone's actions, nor does it imply that you disregard responsibility or boundaries. Rather, it's about letting go of the irrational belief that you can control other people's choices. This stops you from getting frustrated when others don't behave as you want. It makes room for clarity and acceptance, two things that are necessary for developing calm and self-assurance in your life.

Think about a typical situation: last-minute plans being canceled. Anger, a feeling of rejection, or an effort to guilt the individual into rescheduling right away are possible usual reactions. But when you adopt a "Let Them" mentality, you take a moment to acknowledge that others are free to choose what best suits their situation. You respect your time and plans by letting people cancel because you know their choice doesn't reflect your value. You can keep your emotional equilibrium and create opportunities for new activities by letting go of grudges. Handling unwanted criticism or suggestions is another example. Consider a family member who often shares their thoughts on your professional decisions.

The "Let Them" mentality enables you to let people express their thoughts without allowing their comments to control your behavior or undermine your confidence, as opposed to getting into heated disputes or feeling compelled to defend your choices. Their opinion doesn't have to change your course, and accepting their advice frees up energy for your own goals.

This strategy also works in partnerships where limits are frequently pushed. Let's say a friend frequently requests favors but hardly ever gives them back. "Let Them" advises you to establish boundaries for yourself rather than becoming frustrated or trying to alter their conduct. You may choose not to overcommit or provide assistance that you are not truly willing to do. You can break yourself from the cycle of bitterness and martyrdom by letting people behave as they naturally do and concentrating on your own decisions.

The "Let Them" theory can be especially difficult for parents, but it can also be incredibly transformative. For example, many parents attempt to micromanage their children's actions out of concern for their welfare when they get old enough to make decisions on their own. By using "Let Them," parents can learn to trust that their kids will learn from their experiences, even if they make mistakes along the way. This change promotes the child's development and independence while also reducing conflict in the parent-child relationship.

The "Let Them" strategy has an effect in work settings as well. Think about a team member who often misses deadlines, causing frustration. You can concentrate on making sure your contributions match expectations while resolving problems through the proper channels, such as management or delegation, rather than attempting to regulate their work habits or take on their responsibilities. Allowing someone to function as they see fit does not imply that you accept incapacity; rather, it indicates that you will not endure emotional responsibilities that are not yours.

Fundamentally, the "Let Them" mentality stresses self-acceptance and putting your emotional well-being first. This acceptance is a deliberate decision to let go of pointless conflicts; it does not imply apathy or weakness. You develop the ability to choose your battles carefully, saving your energy for the important things. In a romantic relationship, for instance, "Let Them" could indicate allowing your partner to resolve a conflict in their own way rather than demanding that they communicate in the same manner as you. This adaptability lessens conflict and promotes respect for one another.

Understanding that accepting someone for who they are does not mean putting up with negative conduct is a crucial component of this theory. "Let Them" advises you to step back, preserve your serenity, and decide how much access someone has to your life if they consistently disrespect you or transgress your limits. Instead of attempting to mold someone into the person you want them to be, it's about understanding when to let go completely.

Self-awareness and introspection are necessary for the "Let Them" mentality to be used practically. Start by figuring out what aspects of other people's beliefs, decisions, or actions you feel a constant need to control. Consider the reasons for your need and the benefits you expect from exercising control. The underlying motives are frequently based on fear, insecurity, or a need for approval. You can overcome these patterns by recognizing them.

Establishing limits that respect your needs and ideals is another exercise. When you "let them," you're not being a doormat or repressing your emotions. It's about setting boundaries and letting others act as they please. For example, you may resolve not to participate in workplace gossip. Allowing others to gossip without engaging in it does not imply that you support it; rather, it shows that you have a higher standard for yourself and accept their right to behave differently.

Its general applicability to various facets of life is what makes the "Let Them" theory so appealing. It's a way of thinking that can change the dynamics of the workplace as well as interpersonal interactions. By adopting this strategy, you free yourself from the draining responsibility of overseeing the lives of others and acquire the clarity necessary to concentrate on your own objectives and welfare. Allowing people to be who they are is a simple idea, yet it has a significant impact. By reminding you that the only person you really have authority over is yourself, it moves the emphasis from external control to internal empowerment.

People frequently report feeling lighter and having more emotional control when they genuinely embrace the "Let Them" mentality. This change results from the realization that attempting to control the unpredictable is mostly responsible for life's frustration. Letting go does not imply surrender; rather, it signifies a preference for harmony over strife, acceptance over opposition, and assurance over uncertainty. It's about realizing that your value is independent of other people's behavior and that true freedom stems from concentrating on your own ideas, deeds, and choices.

In the end, the "Let Them" mentality is a philosophy for living genuinely, not just a technique for handling relationships. It teaches you to have faith in your own abilities to manage any situation without attempting to exert control over other people. This faith gives you a sense of calm and self-assurance that makes it easier to face life. Allowing them gives you the freedom to be who you are, in addition to allowing others to be who they are.

THE SCIENCE BEHIND LETTING GO

The concept of letting go has deep roots in psychology and neuroscience, offering practical tools for reducing stress and enhancing overall well-being.

Letting go entails letting go of attachment to results, other people's actions, or circumstances that are out of one's control. This mental change is a scientifically proven strategy for leading a happier, more tranquil existence, not just a metaphysical ideal.

Letting go is the act of removing oneself from obsessive thoughts, excessive worry, or unhealthy attachments, according to psychologists. The survival-oriented architecture of the amygdala, the area of the brain in charge of processing emotions, particularly fear and anxiety, is frequently the cause of the brain's propensity to hold onto unpleasant or upsetting ideas. The amygdala remains hyperactive when you obsess over managing other people or results, which prolongs tension and stress. This cycle is broken by letting go, which tells the brain that the perceived threat is no longer important. The prefrontal cortex, which is in charge of rational thought and decision-making, is able to retake control and promote clarity as a result of this change.

Many research studies demonstrate the benefits of letting go in terms of reducing stress. One study from the University of California, Berkeley, for example, discovered that people who accepted their feelings and situation had lower anxiety and despair levels than those who avoided or suppressed emotions. The cognitive load that frequently accompanies unresolved irritation is lessened when one accepts what cannot be altered because it allows the brain to process and release emotions more effectively.

From a neuroscience standpoint, neuroplasticity—the brain's capacity to remodel itself in response to events and behaviors—is associated with letting go. The brain pathways linked to stress responses are weakened, and those linked to composure and flexibility are strengthened when you intentionally decide to let go of a difficult thought or circumstance. This exercise gradually develops a sense of inner stability by teaching your brain to react to difficulties with less emotional response.

This idea is supported by the "Let Them" mentality, which stresses relinquishing control over other people and promotes disengagement from stressors outside of oneself. For instance, you remove a major source of mental stress when you give up trying to influence the conduct of others. This enhances the quality of your relationships in addition to your mental wellness. According to research on interpersonal dynamics, attempting to control others frequently results in resistance and conflict, whereas letting people be themselves fosters an atmosphere of respect and understanding.

The sympathetic (fight-or-flight) and parasympathetic (rest-and-digest) branches of the body's autonomic nervous system are intimately linked to stress and its physiological repercussions. Prolonged stress keeps the sympathetic nervous system active, which can result in problems including high blood pressure, a compromised immune system, and an accelerated heart rate. The parasympathetic nervous system is triggered when you let go, which encourages healing and relaxation. It has been demonstrated that methods like deep breathing and mindfulness, which are frequently linked to the letting-go practice, can lower cortisol levels, lessen inflammation, and enhance general physical health.

Dr. Jon Kabat-Zinn's mindfulness-based stress reduction (MBSR) technique is one useful way to embrace the science of letting go. This method helps people separate from unhelpful thoughts and anxieties by encouraging them to concentrate on the here and now without passing judgment. Research on MBSR has shown that it is a useful tool for people who want to adopt the "Let Them" mentality since it effectively reduces the symptoms of stress, anxiety, and sadness.

Self-determination theory (SDT) is another psychological framework that argues for the advantages of letting go. According to this idea, relatedness, competence, and autonomy are the three fundamental psychological demands of people. You respect people's autonomy when you stop attempting to control them, which improves their sense of self-determination and fortifies your bond with them. This method lessens the stress of overseeing other people's lives, which promotes stronger relationships and improves your own mental health.

The science of letting go also emphasizes how important emotional control is to finding calm and self-assurance. Managing your emotions to conform to your ideals and objectives is known as emotional management. Since it enables you to prioritize what really matters and get rid of things that don't contribute to your well-being, letting go is a type of emotional regulation. For example, you can save mental energy and prevent needless tension by letting go of the reason why someone didn't reply to your message and concentrating on your own priorities.

Positive psychology experts stress the link between developing gratitude and letting go. You make room to enjoy the here-and-now and the good things in your life when you let go of attachment to particular results or expectations. In turn, gratitude improves psychological resilience by reorienting your attention from what is missing to what is abundant. This technique has been demonstrated to improve happiness and lessen depressive symptoms, demonstrating the transformational potential of letting go.

Letting go has significant effects on physical health in addition to psychological ones. Chronic pain, diabetes, and cardiovascular disease have all been related to chronic stress, which is driven by an inability to let go. You may enhance both your physical and emotional health by lowering stress using techniques like acceptance, detachment, and mindfulness. For instance, a study that was published in the journal *Psychosomatic Medicine* revealed that those who used acceptance-based coping mechanisms had reduced levels of inflammation, which is a crucial indicator of diseases linked to stress.

Another important factor backed by science is the part forgiveness plays in letting go. According to studies on forgiveness, letting go of grudges and resentments improves mental health and reduces stress. Forgiveness is about releasing yourself from the emotional weight of resentment and wrath, not about endorsing unacceptable behavior. This is in line with the "Let Them" mentality, which promotes accepting people for who they are without holding them accountable for their deeds.

The importance of letting go of self-judgment has been emphasized by Dr. Kristin Neff, a pioneer in the field of self-compassion research. You can develop a more compassionate and encouraging connection with yourself by letting go of harsh self-criticism and unreasonable expectations. The mental burden of aiming for perfection is lessened, and your confidence is increased by this practice.

The advantages of this way of thinking are further demonstrated by the link between letting go and flow states, a theory made popular by psychologist Mihaly Csikszentmihalyi. When you are completely focused on a task, unaffected by outside distractions or self-consciousness, you are said to be in a state of flow. The conditions for attaining flow, which is linked to increased creativity, productivity, and satisfaction, are created by letting go of internal doubts and external pressures.

WHY CONTROL CREATES STRESS

The desire to control often stems from a natural human need for certainty, security, and predictability. While this instinct can be helpful in specific contexts, such as managing responsibilities or ensuring safety, excessive control frequently creates unintended stress.

Relationships, mental health, and personal growth are severely strained when the desire to handle every aspect of life becomes the norm. Excessive control in relationships shows up as a need to influence the thoughts, actions, or reactions of others. Since most people dislike feeling restricted or micromanaged, this can produce annoyance and conflict. For instance, attempting to sway a friend's choices on their personal or professional lives may appear to be an expression of concern, but it frequently conveys a lack of confidence in their capacity to manage their own situations. This weakens the bond and breeds animosity over time. Controlling behavior weakens the very link it aims to preserve and produces a chasm between people rather than fostering peace.

Anxiety and control are intimately related from a psychological standpoint. According to research, chronic stress levels are frequently higher in those who struggle with excessive control. This is due to the fact that there are intrinsic variables in life that no one can control. People with a high need for control may feel powerless in the face of unpredictable circumstances, which can lead to increased stress reactions. When a child makes decisions that don't align with their expectations, for example, a parent who attempts to micromanage every part of their child's life may find themselves in a state of perpetual stress.

Control also hinders flexibility and receptivity to new experiences, which hinders personal development. Accepting uncertainty and learning from circumstances outside one's control are essential for growth. For example, a person who demands that every aspect of their work be carefully planned may refrain from taking chances, such as investigating a new field or going after an unusual opportunity. The capacity to embrace change as a learning process, build resilience, and uncover new talents is hampered by this inflexible thinking.

The consequences of over-control are further demonstrated by real-world examples. Consider a team leader that micromanages each task that their coworkers are given. Even though their goal may be to guarantee excellent results, this strategy might lead to a restrictive atmosphere where team members feel demotivated and underappreciated. Furthermore, because it becomes unsustainable to constantly monitor every detail, the leader himself/herself is likely to suffer from burnout. In addition to reducing their workload, assigning responsibilities and having faith in others would empower the group and boost productivity.

Perfectionism, a personality trait frequently derived from the urge to control results, is another example of the connection between control and mental health. Persistent discontent and self-criticism result from perfectionists' unreasonably high expectations of both themselves and other people. Research has connected increased levels of anxiety, despair, and burnout to perfectionism. For instance, a student who is obsessed with getting perfect scores may spend endless hours editing, at the expense of their general well-being, social relationships, and sleep. In this instance, the quest for control lowers rather than improves their quality of life.

The inclination to control is further exacerbated by social expectations. Cultural narratives frequently depict those who are able to "keep everything in order" as successful and admirable, equating control with competence. In order to live up to these irrational expectations, people are under pressure to micromanage their lives and those around them. But the truth is that trying to control everything leads to emotional stress and frequently results in feelings of failure when things don't work out as planned.

It is impossible to ignore the physical costs of overcontrol. Chronic stress brought on by an inability to let go is linked to a number of health problems, such as immune system weakness, cardiovascular disease, and hypertension. The fight-or-flight reaction, which is advantageous in brief spurts but detrimental in prolonged durations, is triggered by stress. Conversely, letting go lowers the likelihood of stress-related disorders by allowing the body to regain homeostasis.

The tale of an entrepreneur who tries to manage every facet of their company for years, from marketing tactics to employee conduct, serves as an additional example. The constant pressure to handle every detail has a negative impact on their mental and physical well-being, even though their desire may initially provide results. They might start to feel anxious, have trouble sleeping, or even get physically tired. They discover that their staff feels more empowered, their business keeps growing, and their health improves when they finally assign tasks to others and acknowledge that things won't always go as planned.

It can be freeing to recognize the boundaries of control. Letting go entails realizing what is and is not within one's power to influence; not forgetting obligations; or disregarding significant issues. A fundamental component of emotional intelligence, this distinction enables people to focus their energies on worthwhile endeavors rather than pointless attempts to control the uncontrollable. For example, instead of dwelling on their employer's choices, someone in a challenging work environment can concentrate on developing their abilities or looking for alternative options.

Mindfulness techniques, which stress the value of living in the present, also touch on the idea of control. By encouraging people to analyze their thoughts and feelings objectively, mindfulness aids in their ability to disengage from the need to exert control over their environment. Research on mindfulness has demonstrated that it improves focus, lessens the symptoms of anxiety and sadness, and improves general well-being. People can develop an accepting mindset that is consistent with the tenets of the "Let Them" idea by engaging in mindfulness practices.

As this chapter on comprehending the "Let Them" idea comes to an end, it is evident that the need for control frequently leads to needless stress and impedes personal tranquility. People can release themselves from the weight of irrational expectations and outside pressures by adopting the concept of letting go. This change in perspective promotes better mental health, stronger bonds with others, and more opportunities for personal development. Regaining the energy and focus required to live in peace, confidence, and independence is the goal of mastering the "Let Them" idea, not letting go of accountability.

CHAPTER 2

Redefining Relationships

IDENTIFYING DRAINING RELATIONSHIPS

I dentifying relationships that drain your energy is essential for maintaining your emotional well-being and sense of freedom. The subtle indicators that some relationships are taking more than they are giving are too frequently missed, leaving us feeling emotionally spent, worn out, and undervalued. Living a calm, self-assured, and liberated life requires acknowledging these exhausting dynamics and having the guts to make adjustments.

After engaging with someone, begin by focusing on your feelings. Note your feelings both before and after you spend time with them. Are you feeling exhausted, nervous, or overburdened? Or do you feel energized, encouraged, and supported? The energy you leave after a connection can indicate its nurturing or draining nature. A relationship may be draining if you frequently feel worn out, empty, or sad after interacting with someone.

The ongoing need for emotional work is one of the main indicators of a depleting relationship. Certain people in your life may expect you to always listen, solve, or cheer them up. Supporting those we care about is natural, but partnerships should be mutually beneficial. It's an indication that the needs of one person have taken precedence over your own if you find yourself constantly giving without ever getting the same amount of care or attention in return. This one-sided relationship might eventually cause anger and frustration.

A lack of regard for one another is another crucial sign. Respect is the foundation of healthy relationships, where both parties respect one another's time, space, emotions, and boundaries. It's an indication that the relationship is not based on mutual respect if you are frequently interrupted, ignored, or denigrated. Ignoring your needs or feelings can lead to a toxic environment that drains your energy and damages your sense of value.

Another positive sign that a relationship is unhealthy is if you feel like you have to be cautious around someone all the time. People with volatile or unpredictable behaviors are frequently involved in relationships that drain you. This might cause anxiety and cause you to continuously question your words or behavior to avoid offending them or causing disagreement. You experience tension and apprehension rather than relaxation and ease. Over time, this feeling of having to tread carefully can lead to emotional tiredness since you are always attempting to keep the peace or prevent offending people.

When someone consistently brings negativity into your life, that's another clue. Everyone experiences difficult times, but some people appear to spend most of their time complaining, criticizing, and focusing on their problems rather than trying to solve them or do anything. It's an indication that the connection is draining your energy into a negative area if you find that your chats are frequently negative, whether they are about relationships, jobs, or life in general. Even though you could feel burdened by their difficulties after every chat, they never appear to want to alter their viewpoint or accept accountability for their deeds. Feeling depleted and powerless might result from persistent negativity without a desire to change.

The idea of emotional manipulation is a crucial one to comprehend. Some people can drain your energy by making you feel like you owe them something, guilty, or responsible for their happiness. To achieve their goals, they might play the victim, guilt-trip, or employ passive-aggressive remarks. In addition to undermining your self-esteem, these manipulative actions foster an unhealthy relationship in which you feel pressured to offer more than you are capable of. A relationship is exhausting if you ever feel like you're balancing on a tightrope, attempting to please someone to prevent conflict or their unfavorable reactions.

The incapacity to enjoy your victories or triumphs is a subtle but significant indicator. A draining individual may minimize your accomplishments or make you feel negative about them. Instead of encouraging or celebrating your successes, they may be jealous or indifferent, indicating a problem in the relationship. Instead of being minimized or disregarded, you ought to feel encouraged and honored in your development.

The absence of personal development is another significant element. Relationships that drain you often prevent you from being your best self. They might discourage or minimize your desires rather than urging you to follow your passions, objectives, or aspirations. Through overt or covert criticism, they foster an atmosphere that makes progress seem unattainable or undesirable. Maintaining the self-assurance and drive required to follow your dreams becomes more challenging when you are not assisted in your personal growth. Here is a list of indicators to watch out for in order to determine whether a relationship is draining:

1. Emotional exhaustion following interactions: After interacting with this individual, do you feel exhausted, nervous, or angry?

2. One-sided emotional labor: Do you constantly listen to their issues without offering any kind of support or caring in return?

3. Inconsideration: Do they neglect your time, limits, or feelings?

4. Walking on eggshells: Are you hesitant or scared to express your opinions or be yourself in their presence?

5. Persistent negativity: Do the discussions mostly center on grievances, issues, or the undesirable things in life?

6. Emotional manipulation: Do you hold yourself accountable or feel negative about their contentment or welfare?

7. Ignore your success: When you triumph, do they display jealousy or minimize your accomplishments?

8. Discouragement of personal development: Do they give you the impression that your aspirations are unworthy or unreachable?

It's crucial to stand back and evaluate the connection if any of these warning signs apply to your own experiences. According to the Let Them philosophy, maintaining your calm and vitality in relationships requires letting go of control and expectations. You can begin making deliberate decisions about where to spend your time and energy by identifying the warning signals of draining relationships.

You can have a better understanding of the connections in your life by engaging in practical exercises. Start by jotting down the names of the persons you frequently communicate with. After spending time with each person, write down your feelings. Do you feel energized and elevated, or do you feel exhausted and empty? You can use this activity to find trends and relationships that require extra care or boundaries.

Writing in a journal about your emotions following particular encounters might also provide understanding. Write about a conversation that left you feeling emotionally spent, for example. What particular acts or behaviors triggered this emotion? Was it their persistent whining, their lack of assistance, or their deceptive behavior? You might create plans for managing future interactions or establishing limits by identifying the precise reasons behind your uneasiness.

Applying the Let Them strategy to your everyday life is equally beneficial. While you have no control over others' actions, you do have full control over how much energy they drain from you. In addition to deciding what you will and won't put up with in your relationships, you can also choose to accept them for who they are. This change in perspective enables you to maintain positive, healthy relationships while conserving your energy and tranquility.

Recall that the secret to spotting toxic relationships is to pay attention to how encounters make you feel. You can begin building relationships that uplift and encourage you by identifying the warning signs and establishing reasonable limits. The Let Them hypothesis offers a potent foundation for changing the way you think about relationships, enabling you to set aside unneeded expectations and concentrate on what is actually best for your well-being.

These useful activities, examples, and writing prompts will help you use the Let Them Principle to detect depleting relationships by getting you to think about and evaluate their interactions. These exercises can help you identify toxic relationships and establish limits to protect their tranquility, autonomy, and self-esteem.

EXERCISE 1: EMOTIONAL CHECK-IN AFTER INTERACTIONS

Objective: To assess how different relationships affect your energy and well-being.

1. After any meaningful interaction (phone call, meeting, or text conversation), take a moment to check in with yourself.

2. Ask: **How do I feel?** Are you energized, happy, and light, or do you feel drained, anxious, or frustrated?

3. Record your feelings in a notebook or journal. Focus on:

- Whether you felt emotionally supported or dismissed.
- Whether you felt free to express yourself or had to walk on eggshells.
- If the interaction left you feeling better or worse.

Example:

You had a lunch with a friend who constantly talks about their problems but never seems to offer support when you share yours. You leave feeling emotionally exhausted and unimportant. In your journal, write down:

- "I felt drained and unheard."
- "I realize I do most of the emotional labor in this relationship."

EXERCISE 2: RELATIONSHIP ENERGY MAPPING

Objective: To visually assess the balance of energy exchange in your relationships.

1. Draw a circle in the center of a page and write your name in it.

2. Around the circle, write down the names of people you interact with regularly (family, friends, colleagues, etc.).

3. For each person, note whether they add energy to your life (positive, supportive) or drain it (negative, unsupportive). Use symbols or color codes like:

- + for those who energize you.
- - for those who drain you.

4. Look at the overall picture. Is there a balance? Are there more negative symbols than positive?

Example:

You might notice that most of your relationships are marked with a "-" symbol. This could be a red flag that it's time to evaluate how much energy you're investing in relationships that do not give back.

EXERCISE 3: THE ACCOUNTABILITY LIST

Objective: To assess who in your life takes responsibility for their actions and who does not.

1. Write down the names of people who regularly impact your life.

2. For each person, answer the following questions:

- Do they take responsibility for their emotions and actions?
- Do they consistently blame you or others for their problems?

- Are they willing to work on themselves and grow, or do they resist change?

3. Reflect on how these answers make you feel. Do certain people leave you feeling like you're constantly taking on their emotional burden?

Example:

If a friend constantly complains about their job but never takes action to improve their situation, you might feel frustrated and powerless. Journal your thoughts:

- "This friend rarely takes responsibility for their own happiness. I feel like I'm expected to solve their problems."

EXERCISE 4: SET BOUNDARIES WITH ONE DRAINING PERSON

Objective: To practice applying the Let Them Principle by establishing healthy boundaries.

1. Choose one relationship that feels draining.

2. Reflect on what specific behaviors from this person are causing you stress. Is it their constant negativity, their need for emotional support without reciprocation, or their lack of respect for your time?

3. Set a clear boundary with that person. It could be:

- Limiting the amount of time you spend together.
- Redirecting conversations away from their problems when you've already offered support.
- Letting them know when their behavior is crossing a line and how it affects you.

4. Record your feelings about this process. Were you able to set the boundary without guilt or fear?

Example:

You decide to set a boundary with a colleague who constantly dumps their emotional problems on you. You tell them, "I understand you're having a tough time, but I need to focus on my own work right now. I'll check in with you later when I have the space." Journal:

- "Setting this boundary felt freeing. I didn't feel guilty—just empowered."

EXERCISE 5: THE "GUILT-FREE NO" PRACTICE

Objective: To become more comfortable saying "no" without feeling guilty.

1. Choose a day to practice saying "no" to requests, invitations, or obligations that feel draining or that you simply don't have the energy for.

2. Reflect on how it feels to say "no" and whether you feel any guilt or fear afterward. If you do, acknowledge those feelings and remind yourself that saying "no" is necessary for protecting your emotional health.

3. Journal about your experience:

- What did you say "no" to?
- How did it feel afterward? Did your energy improve?
- Did you notice any guilt, and how did you handle it?

Example:

You receive an invitation to a social event that you don't feel like attending. Instead of going because you feel obligated, you politely decline. Journal:

- "I said no to the event without feeling guilty. I realized I need to prioritize my own peace right now."

JOURNALING PROMPT 1: ASSESSING EMOTIONAL DRAINAGE

Objective: To increase awareness of how specific people affect your emotional state.

- Think about the last time you spent time with someone who drained you. What happened during the interaction? How did you feel afterward?
- Were there moments in the interaction where you felt dismissed, unheard, or emotionally exhausted?
- Write about the behavior you found most draining, and how you could set boundaries in the future to protect your emotional energy.

JOURNALING PROMPT 2: EVALUATING EMOTIONAL RESPONSIBILITY

Objective: To identify who in your life takes responsibility for their emotions.

- Reflect on the people closest to you. Do they take ownership of their feelings and actions, or do they often blame others for their emotional state?
- How do these dynamics affect your own emotional well being? Do you feel responsible for fixing their emotions?

- Write about how you can shift your own perspective to let others manage their own feelings while protecting your emotional space.

JOURNALING PROMPT 3: RECOGNIZING THE NEED FOR CHANGE

Objective: To reflect on whether a relationship needs to change.

- Think about a draining relationship in your life. What would happen if you let go of expectations and simply allowed the other person to "be" without trying to fix them, change them, or meet their emotional demands?
- What would it feel like to embrace the Let Them Principle in this relationship? How could you shift your energy from guilt or frustration to peace and acceptance?
- Journal about the changes you might need to make to regain emotional freedom and confidence in this relationship.

You can recognize unhealthy relationships and begin the process of replacing them with more balanced, healthy ones with the help of these activities, reflections, and suggestions. The first step in letting go of control, as suggested by the Let Them Principle, is identifying the areas where your energy is being diverted and consciously choosing to keep your peace. You can make more room in your life for happiness, self-assurance, and genuine connection by being deliberate about your emotional health and boundaries.

LET THEM BE: BUILDING BOUNDARIES WITH EASE

Maintaining mental clarity, emotional stability, and personal calm all depend on having appropriate boundaries. In the realm of relationships, whether with partners, family, friends, or coworkers, it's simple to fall into the trap of trying to please everyone or feeling bad about voicing your demands. However, you may empower yourself to safeguard your time, energy, and mental well-being by understanding how to establish clear limits. The boundaries you set allow you to live intentionally and authentically, not separate you.

When we discuss "letting them be" in relation to limits, we are emphasizing the fact that each person has a distinct manner of being and acting. Accepting people as they are and not trying to change them gives limits power. Managing your reaction to their behavior is more important than controlling it. The secret to preserving your tranquility, independence, and self-assurance is striking this equilibrium.

Realizing that your needs and wants are as essential as anyone else's is the first step toward setting boundaries with ease. If something doesn't serve you or fit your values, say no. Setting boundaries can be a difficult concept, particularly if you are not accustomed to putting your own health first. However, it gets easier with practice, and you'll soon discover that maintaining your peace doesn't have to mean feeling guilty.

The fear of disappointing other people is one of the most frequent causes of boundary issues. "If I say no, they will be upset with me," or "What if they stop liking me?" are mental voices that we have all heard. Although it's normal to fear rejection, those who care about you will respect your boundaries. The people who drain your energy are probably the ones who don't. Setting boundaries entails having the confidence to stand up for yourself in ways you haven't in the past.

You must first define what you need and what you won't tolerate to set guilt-free limits. This entails being aware of your feelings toward particular persons or circumstances. After some encounters, do you frequently feel overburdened, exhausted, or anxious? It's time to accept those emotions and take preventative measures. Begin by posing these queries to yourself:

- What situations or behaviors make me feel uncomfortable, angry, or anxious?
- Which relationships leave me feeling exhausted or unappreciated?
- What do I need to feel safe, respected, and supported?

It's time to express your boundaries once you've gained a better grasp of them. It is important to convey boundaries in a straightforward, sincere, and polite manner. For instance, you could respond, "I like helping you, but I also need some time for myself," if a buddy is always requesting favors but never offers to help you in return. This time, I won't be able to assist." A sentence like this is forceful but kind. It expresses your needs without criticizing or assaulting the other individual.

Learning to say no without going into too much detail or offering an apology is another aspect of setting boundaries. You don't have to provide an explanation or defend your choice. "I'm sorry, I can't," or "I'm not available," is sufficient. The important thing is to speak it guilt-free and with confidence. Keep in mind that you are saying no to your own well-being each time you accept something that doesn't benefit you.

You could initially encounter opposition from both yourself and other people. If you're used to being more accommodating or available, people may push back against your new boundaries and test your new "no." This indicates that you're doing things correctly and is normal. Maintaining consistency is crucial. People will respect your boundaries when you stand your ground, and you will become more comfortable voicing your requirements.

It's essential to follow through in order to preserve these boundaries. Setting boundaries is a commitment to yourself, not a recommendation. You're giving the wrong impression if you set a limit with a coworker about not working after hours but then let them continue to text or contact you at odd hours. Setting and upholding limits calls for consistency and discipline. Reminding yourself that you teach others how to treat you when you respect your needs helps.

Take a minute to consider why you set the limit in the first place if you catch yourself sliding or when remorse begins to seep in. Is the individual or circumstance truly worth letting go of your tranquility for? Which is more important: satisfying the other person or protecting your own mental health? You can avoid feeling conflicted and maintain your strength by restating your justifications for the limit.

Establishing boundaries also entails knowing how to respond when they are crossed. For instance, it's crucial to confront someone directly if they keep interrupting you while you're speaking: "I'd appreciate it if you let me finish my thought before responding." Without coming across as unduly combative, this style of straightforward communication guarantees that your boundaries are respected.

Self-care is another essential component of establishing boundaries. You make room for pursuits and connections that truly make you feel better when you set clear boundaries. Enforcing your boundaries with others is vital, but so are other things, like sleeping, taking time for a hobby, or spending more time with individuals who make you feel good. Setting boundaries involves more than just saying "no" to other people; it also involves saying "yes" to oneself.

Understanding and reiterating your boundaries might be facilitated by keeping a journal. You can stay rooted in your ideals and make sense of your demands by thinking back on your experiences. For instance, you could write in your notebook about how it felt to have to set boundaries during a challenging conversation: Was it initially uncomfortable but then empowering? Did they respect your boundaries? What changes can you make to your strategy the next time?

Managing guilt or the fear of offending someone is one of the most difficult aspects of setting boundaries. Try rephrasing your viewpoint to counter this: How other people respond to your limits is not your responsibility. Limiting others honors their needs as well as yours. Boundaries are the cornerstone of mutual respect, which is the foundation of healthy partnerships. It's crucial to engage in self-compassion exercises to strengthen your limits. Understand that establishing limits is a skill that requires practice. You could experience feelings of guilt or uncertainty at times, but this is a normal part of the process. You are coming closer to building the life you genuinely desire— one in which you feel strong, self-assured, and content—each time you make an effort to assert yourself.

In conclusion, learning to respect your own needs Guilt-free is the key to setting boundaries with ease. It's about realizing your well-being is as important as anyone else's and letting go of disappointing others. Setting and upholding limits will become more natural the more you do it. Doing this will give you more peace, independence, and self-confidence. The technique of "letting them be," or letting others be who they are while preserving your own emotional space, may be mastered by taking persistent action. According to the Let Them Principle, this is the cornerstone of leading a genuine and courageous life.

PRACTICAL EXERCISES

Here are practical exercises, examples, and journaling prompts to help you apply the Let Them Principle when building boundaries with ease:

EXERCISE 1: IDENTIFYING YOUR BOUNDARIES

- Take a moment to reflect on your daily life and interactions. Write down situations or people that consistently leave you feeling drained, stressed, or overwhelmed.
- Ask yourself: "What behaviors, requests, or habits do I need to set clear boundaries around?"
- For each item, write a simple statement of the boundary you need to set. For example, "I will no longer respond to work emails after 6 PM."

EXERCISE 2: SAYING NO WITHOUT GUILT

- Next time someone asks something of you that you don't want to do, practice saying no. Start small. It could be as simple as declining a social invitation or saying no to an additional task at work.

- After saying no, write down how you felt. Did guilt arise? Did you feel empowered or anxious?
- Reflect on why saying no was important and how it contributed to your peace of mind.

EXERCISE 3: BOUNDARY REINFORCEMENT

- Identify a recurring boundary challenge in your life. It might be a person who constantly interrupts you or a friend who demands more of your time than you're willing to give.
- Create a strategy for addressing this boundary. This could involve a direct conversation or setting limits in your interactions. Write down the key phrases you can use, like, "I need to take some time for myself today," or "I can't take on any more work right now."
- Practice these phrases aloud until they feel natural. The goal is to respond with calm and confidence, without guilt.

Example:

Let's say you have a friend who frequently asks for favors without offering help in return. You've been feeling taken advantage of but haven't said anything. Using the Let Them Principle, you realize that you're not responsible for changing your friend's behavior, but you can set a boundary.

- You might say, "I love helping you, but I also need to take care of myself. I won't be able to help this time." By being clear and direct, you reinforce your boundary and free yourself from unnecessary guilt.

EXERCISE 4: PRACTICING SELF-COMPASSION

- It's common to feel guilt when you first start setting boundaries. To counteract this, practice self-compassion. Write a compassionate letter to yourself. Acknowledge that learning to set boundaries is a growth process.
- Example: "Dear Me, I know it can be hard to say no, but I am proud of the steps I'm taking to protect my peace. I am worthy of respect, and it's okay to prioritize myself."

EXERCISE 5: CHECK-IN JOURNAL

- Set aside time at the end of each week to reflect on your boundary-setting progress. Write down:
- Instances where you successfully enforced a boundary.
- How it made you feel.

- Any challenges you faced and how you overcame them.
- Over time, this journal will help you track your growth and identify areas where you might need additional practice.

JOURNALING PROMPTS FOR CLARITY:

1. What boundaries do I struggle with the most? Why?

2. What are the signs I'm starting to feel overwhelmed or drained by someone or something?

3. When I say "yes" to others, what am I saying "no" to for myself?

4. How does setting a boundary help me maintain my peace and mental clarity?

5. Write about a time when you felt guilty for setting a boundary. How can you reframe this experience as an act of self-care?

Example Scenario for Reflection:

You've been invited to a family event, but you're already feeling overwhelmed with work and need some rest. In the past, you might have attended the event out of obligation, but now you're practicing boundary-setting. You decide to politely decline, giving yourself the space to rest.

Afterwards, journal about how it felt to prioritize your needs and how it will impact your well-being in the long run. Did you feel guilty? Did you feel relief?

REFLECTION EXERCISE FOR PERSONAL GROWTH:

- Reflect on how your relationships have been affected by your boundary-setting. Have people started respecting your limits? Are there some relationships that have become more balanced?
- Write down any shifts you've noticed in your energy levels, mental clarity, or overall sense of peace since you started setting boundaries.

By practicing these exercises and journaling prompts, you will gradually build the muscle of setting boundaries with ease. Over time, it will become second nature to protect your peace without guilt, empowering you to live with more confidence and freedom.

HOW TO RECOGNIZE AND NURTURE HEALTHY CONNECTIONS

Building serenity, freedom, and confidence in your life requires identifying and fostering healthy relationships. Inspired by Mel Robbins' teachings, the Let Them Principle provides a potent framework for comprehending how to cultivate these relationships without feeling burdened, guilty, or accountable for the feelings or deeds of others. It teaches us that by letting individuals be who they are but still upholding a strong sense of peace and self-respect, we may create meaningful connections. Mutual respect, trust, understanding, and open communication are traits of healthy relationships.

You should be lifted up, not drained, by these relationships. A few essential characteristics should be evident while identifying these linkages. The first essential component of a positive relationship is the capacity to speak honestly and freely without worrying about criticism or reprisal. Both people feel heard and appreciated in partnerships that are helpful. Active listening is just as important to communication as speaking. This is exactly in line with the Let Them Principle, which permits you to express your truth while honoring the truth of others. You make room for genuine conversation when you practice accepting others for who they are, without feeling the need to alter or control them. For example, if a buddy confides in you about an issue they're having, you should feel free to give your assistance without feeling pressured to solve it. They should also honor your wants without attempting to resolve your problems.

Respect for one another is another crucial trait. Understanding that everyone has their own thoughts, feelings, and limits is key to healthy relationships. One of the most important aspects of the Let Them Principle is respecting boundaries. Allowing people to be themselves—whether that means giving them space or letting them express themselves—you value them. At the same time, you establish a space where both people feel appreciated by establishing your own boundaries and honoring theirs. For instance, a friend who understands your need for solitude doesn't make you feel negative about it; instead, they encourage your self-care routines. Likewise, the friendship is strengthened when you respect their boundaries without attempting to cross them.

Another essential component of wholesome partnerships is trust. In a relationship based on trust, both parties are aware that they can rely on each other—not always, but in significant ways. Over time, this trust is established by constant behavior that demonstrates dependability and integrity. By not pressuring or dictating how the connection develops, you can use the Let Them Principle to let trust develop organically. Rather, you just show up, communicate your wants, and allow the connection to develop naturally without coercion or pressure. Deepening any connection requires both sides to feel comfortable being vulnerable, which is made possible by this trust.

A vital component of fostering wholesome relationships is emotional support. It's critical to understand that providing emotional support does not entail bearing the weight of another person's feelings. Rather, it entails demonstrating compassion, lending a sympathetic ear, and providing support when required. You can help someone without bearing their emotional burden, according to the Let Them Principle. Allowing both people to express their feelings without feeling obligated to solve one another's problems is a sign of a good partnership. Allowing someone to be allows you to respect their independence while providing consolation from a point of empathy.

Shared growth is another characteristic of helpful relationships. Healthy relationships create a setting where both people support each other's growth. The connection encourages both parties to develop both personally and collectively rather than being mired in outdated routines or habits. When applying the Let Them Principle, you recognize that others have their own paths. While focusing on yourself, you can support their development without feeling insecure. For instance, encouraging a close friend who is taking up a new career or activity, even if it means they may become busier or more independent, is a healthy reaction. Instead of seeing their success as a mark against yours, use it to improve.

After you've determined what makes a relationship healthy, it's critical to actively cultivate it. The Let Them Principle offers us a straightforward yet effective method for doing this.

Making room for positive connections is the first step in fostering them. Relationships cannot flourish in settings that are demanding, controlling, or predetermined. You allow your relationships to develop organically by putting the Let Them Principle into practice. It's not necessary to strive to mold the connection in a particular way or force intimacy. Allow individuals to approach you in their own time and manner. Both sides can feel more at ease, and genuine connections are fostered by this technique.

A fundamental tenet of this is to refrain from attempting to alter others. When both people are able to be real, healthy partnerships flourish. The Let Them

Principle promotes letting go of the need to correct other people, control their actions, or force your own beliefs on them. The bond grows stronger when you accept someone for who they are without feeling compelled to change them. For instance, you can accept a friend's tendency to be unorganized or late without feeling the need to continuously reprimand them. Consider their positive contributions to the partnership rather than their flaws.

Forgiveness must be practiced in addition to accepting others. Every relationship has its share of misunderstandings and arguments since nobody is flawless. The friendship can continue to develop if you practice forgiveness and let go of grudges. According to the Let Them Principle, forgiveness does not entail allowing others to treat you badly or disregarding your boundaries. Instead, it implies that you let go of grudges and let the relationship grow without the burden of past transgressions. For example, forgive rather than resent when a close friend fails to remember a significant occasion or disappoints you in some other way. Admit mistakes are inevitable and use the opportunity to have a calm conversation about the issue to improve the relationship.

The practice of self-awareness is also crucial. Being aware of your own wants, feelings, and limits is essential to fostering wholesome relationships. The Let Them Principle will help you prioritize your needs while still helping others. It's easy to get caught up in others' needs. This calls for consistent introspection and being truthful with yourself about your needs in a relationship. For example, if a conversation leaves you feeling emotionally spent, accept it and allow yourself time to recover. However, in order for you and your friend to maintain a positive relationship, don't be afraid to speak openly about your desire for balance.

Maintaining successful relationships also heavily relies on courteous and consistent communication. In addition to resolving disputes, open communication improves your relationship. You create room for mutual understanding when you express your feelings and thoughts. By using the Let Them Principle, you may communicate your ideas clearly while also being open to hearing what others have to say. Trust and a sense of security are fostered by this giving and receiving equilibrium.

Lastly, it's critical to comprehend the significance of both giving and receiving. As important as it is to support and encourage others, healthy relationships require reciprocity. By letting others provide support or guidance when required, the Let Them Principle encourages you to embrace vulnerability. The relationship between you and the other person is strengthened when you accept support politely and without hesitation.

In conclusion, mutual respect, communication, trust, and development are the foundations of wholesome partnerships. According to the Let Them Principle, you should cultivate acceptance, relinquish control, and make room for real connections. By concentrating on fostering these connections with integrity, compassion, and kindness, you may build a network of support that enables you to live a calm, independent, and self-assured life. These relationships, which are based on respect and gratitude for one another, can not only improve your life but also aid your personal development and interpersonal growth.

PRACTICAL EXERCISES

Here are practical exercises, examples, and journaling prompts to help you recognize and nurture healthy relationships using the Let Them Principle:

1. EXERCISE: IDENTIFYING HEALTHY CONNECTIONS

Write down the names of your closest friends, family members, and colleagues. For each person, ask yourself:

- Do I feel heard and understood in this relationship?
- Do I feel supported without being pressured to change?
- Do we both respect each other's boundaries and needs?

Are there any patterns or red flags?

Example: Practicing Letting People Be

Think of someone in your life whose behavior or emotions you've tried to control. The next time you interact with this person, consciously practice the Let Them Principle by allowing them to express themselves without jumping in to fix things or offer solutions. Notice how this changes the dynamic and how it feels to simply let them be who they are.

EXERCISE: COMMUNICATION CHECK

Healthy relationships thrive on open communication. Write down a recent conversation you had with someone close to you. Ask yourself:

- Did I speak honestly without fear of judgment or retaliation?
- Did I listen actively to their needs or feelings?
- Was there space for both of us to be heard?

Use this to assess how effectively you're communicating. In the future, aim to create more space for honest dialogue without interrupting or silencing each other.

JOURNALING PROMPT: SELF-REFLECTION ON BOUNDARIES

Reflect on your current relationships and ask yourself:

- Are there any relationships where I feel my boundaries are being crossed or ignored?
- How do I feel after spending time with certain people? Energized, drained, or neutral?

Write about specific instances where you've had to enforce or wish you had enforced a boundary. What might have changed if you had done so with more confidence? How can you apply the Let Them Principle to protect your boundaries while nurturing these relationships?

EXERCISE: THE SUPPORT CHALLENGE

Write down one person in your life who often seeks emotional support from you. Reflect on whether you feel genuinely able to support them, or if you feel burdened or overwhelmed. The next time this person reaches out, practice offering empathy without taking on their emotional burden. Offer your support, but let them handle their own emotional journey.

Example: Celebrating Others' Successes

Think of someone in your life who has recently achieved something significant. Instead of feeling threatened, take a moment to celebrate their success. Write them a message of congratulations or express your genuine pride in their accomplishment. Recognizing their growth while focusing on your own will help you nurture a healthy, supportive relationship without comparison or insecurity.

JOURNALING PROMPT: GROWTH TOGETHER

Think about a relationship where you and the other person have grown or evolved together. Write about the changes you've both experienced and how those changes have contributed to the strength of the relationship. How can you continue to support each other's growth while staying true to your individual needs?

EXERCISE: FORGIVENESS PRACTICE

Reflect on a time when you felt wronged or hurt by someone close to you. Write down your feelings and the impact it had on the relationship. Now, practice forgiveness by writing a letter (you don't have to send) where you express your feelings honestly and release any resentment. Recognize that forgiveness is about freeing yourself to grow, not condoning bad behavior.

JOURNALING PROMPT: LETTING GO OF CONTROL

Write about a relationship where you've tried to control the other person's actions, thoughts, or feelings. How did that affect the relationship? Did it bring you peace or frustration? Reflect on how practicing the Let Them Principle would change the dynamic. What does it look like to release the need to control, while still fostering connection?

EXERCISE: ENERGY CHECK

Each time you interact with a close friend or loved one, take a moment afterward to assess how you feel. Do you feel uplifted and energized? Or drained and exhausted? Make a note of the interactions that leave you feeling good and those that leave you feeling bad. Pay attention to any patterns and take action to nurture the relationships that energize you, while gently creating distance from those that drain you.

By actively using these exercises and prompts, you can start to recognize and nurture healthy connections in alignment with the Let Them Principle. Healthy relationships are based on mutual respect, trust, and understanding, and the more you practice letting others be themselves while maintaining your own boundaries, the more you will experience peace, freedom, and confidence in your connections.

CHAPTER 3

Mastering Emotional Freedom

BREAKING FREE FROM PEOPLE'S OPINIONS

I n a world where social media and personal interactions can leave us feeling judged and criticized, it is easy to become overly concerned with other people's opinions. The weight of other people's opinions can frequently feel oppressive, whether it comes from a family member's remark, an unsolicited piece of advice from a friend, or a casual remark from a complete stranger. Understanding that your identity is not defined by the views of others is the first step toward escaping this tendency. When you stop allowing outside influences to shape your decisions and sense of value, you will experience true inner peace, independence, and confidence.

Many people suffer from the desire for outside approval, thinking that they are acting morally if others agree with their views or behaviors. This has its roots in our social conditioning, which is the need to be liked or accepted. We learn early on to look for approval from friends, parents, and teachers. This urge can develop into an excessive need to please others as we get older, frequently at the price of our own genuineness. We lose sight of who we are and what we really want when we let other people's opinions influence our choices.

Accepting that people's opinions are simply that—opinions—is the first step towards ending this loop. They are predicated on other people's viewpoints, experiences, and beliefs, which are frequently constrained and could not coincide with your own values or life goals. In actuality, nobody else is experiencing your reality, walking in your shoes, or going through your path.

Their views don't define you and shouldn't shape your life. It's important to start by developing self-awareness in order to start releasing yourself from the burden of other people's opinions. Step back and consider why you care about other people's opinions. Does their viewpoint stem from something positive, or is it merely a mirror of their own anxieties and fears? Detaching yourself from external affirmation will be easier the more you get why you value it so highly. Self-awareness helps you distinguish between your own and others' pressures.

Setting limits is the next step when you have a better grasp of why other people's opinions impact you. People frequently impose their own values and beliefs on other people without considering the possibility that what suits them might not fit you. You have the right to politely end a conversation or even leave if someone is giving you unwelcome advice or criticism that doesn't support your objectives. You don't have to provide anyone an explanation for your decision to live your life as you see fit. Establishing boundaries entails keeping your peace and putting your health before other people's comfort.

Another essential element of escaping the influence of others is developing self-confidence in your decisions. Knowing who you are and having faith in your capacity to make choices that are consistent with your values and desires are the foundations of confidence. You can strengthen your sense of independence and self-worth by practicing making decisions based on your own needs and intuition. Knowing that only you write your story boosts your confidence. Every choice you make, no matter how big or small, is a chance to take charge of your life and validate your self-worth.

Realizing that not everyone will agree with you and that that's okay is another crucial component of overcoming the influence of other people's opinions. Actually, attempting to win over everyone is a definite way to lose your identity. People will always disagree with you or hold an unfavorable opinion, regardless of how hard you try. This is only a fact of life and does not represent your value. You will feel more free the sooner you realize that happiness does not depend on everyone's approval.

Analyzing the opinion's origin can also be beneficial. Think about whether the person expressing their opinion is acting in your best interests or projecting their own insecurities. People who are judgmental or critical frequently do so as a result of their own unresolved issues or anxieties. Recognize that what people say may reveal more about them than about you, so don't take it personally. By changing your viewpoint, you can cease internalizing these beliefs and see them for what they are: a viewpoint held by another person, not an objective assessment of your value.

The first step in letting go of the need for other people's approval is learning to trust yourself. Listen to your inner voice first. What is it that you truly desire? No matter what others think, what's best for you? Our intuition is frequently muffled by the voice of our inner critic, but we can begin to hear our actual wants more clearly by engaging in self-reflection and mindfulness exercises. The more you respect and listen to yourself, the less power outside opinions have.

Understanding that you may make mistakes is one of the most freeing habits. Too frequently, people put off making choices or acting because they are afraid of what other people will think if they don't succeed. But failing is a necessary component of learning and development. You start to take more chances and follow your dreams without hesitation when you stop worrying about criticism or failure. Whether it's a success or a failure, every event turns into a worthwhile lesson that boosts your self-esteem and develops your faith in your own judgment.

You can start cultivating appreciation for your individuality to support these mental shifts. Take a moment to recognize the traits, values, and strengths that define you every time you feel pressured to fit in or concerned about how other people see you. Celebrate the truth that you are special because you are unique and that you are not supposed to fit into any mold. You can start to change the way you see yourself by turning your attention from getting praise from others to getting it from yourself.

Limiting your exposure to people or situations that constantly reinforce your fears or make you doubt yourself is another useful strategy. It might be time to reevaluate your interactions with friends, coworkers, or social media profiles if they consistently make you feel inferior. Spend time with people who accept you and inspire you to be your best without judging you.

It takes constant self-empowerment to break free from other people's opinions; it doesn't happen suddenly. You regain your strength every time you decide to put your own voice above criticism from others. As you develop the muscle of trust and self-assurance, other people's opinions will become less significant over time. In the end, your own views are the most significant in your life. Respecting your truth makes room for confidence, independence, and serenity to permeate every aspect of your existence.

You can progressively break free from the influence of other people's opinions by putting these measures into practice. You'll begin to view your life from your own perspective rather than the skewed perspectives of others. This perspective shift will allow you to live your life as you are, not as others want you to be, and realize your full potential without judgment.

Here are some useful activities, examples, and writing prompts that support the ideas in "Mastering the Power of Let Them: A No Nonsense Guide to Peace, Freedom, and Confidence" and will assist you in releasing the burden of other people's opinions. These exercises can help you prioritize being true to yourself, reclaim your inner power, and let go of the need for approval from others.

1. EXERCISE: IDENTIFY AND CHALLENGE YOUR FEARS

Start by identifying specific fears or concerns you have about what others might think of you. Are you avoiding a decision because of someone else's opinion? Write it down. Then, challenge the fear:

- What's the worst that could happen if I follow my own choice?
- Who does this decision impact the most: me or others?
- How does living by others' opinions hold me back?

Journaling Prompt: "What is a recent decision I hesitated to make because of someone else's opinion? What was the actual outcome when I moved forward with my own decision?"

2. EXERCISE: BUILD YOUR INNER SUPPORT SYSTEM

Instead of relying on external opinions, create a support system within yourself. Visualize your most confident and empowered self. How would this version of you respond to others' judgments or criticism?

- Sit quietly and imagine a version of yourself that feels no need for approval.
- Write down what advice your empowered self would give you when someone's opinion starts affecting your choices.

Journaling Prompt: "When I feel the weight of someone else's opinion, how can I tap into my inner strength to make a decision that aligns with my true self?"

3. EXERCISE: REFRAME NEGATIVE SELF-TALK

Often, the opinions of others trigger negative self-talk. When you notice yourself engaging in this kind of thinking, pause and reframe it. Instead of thinking "I'm doing this because others expect it," shift to "I am doing this because it aligns with my values."

Journaling Prompt: "What is one situation where I've been influenced by someone else's opinion? How can I reframe that situation to focus on my values?"

4. EXERCISE: SET BOUNDARIES FOR EXTERNAL INFLUENCE

A big part of breaking free from others' opinions is setting clear boundaries. Reflect on the areas of your life where you may have allowed others' opinions to dominate. Decide to implement boundaries where necessary. If you're not comfortable with someone's feedback, it's okay to say no or walk away.

- Create a simple script to help you set boundaries with people who tend to impose their opinions on you.

Example Script: "I appreciate your input, but I've decided to move forward with my own decision."

Journaling Prompt: "What is a boundary I can implement to protect my peace when someone imposes their opinion on me?"

5. EXERCISE: CELEBRATE YOUR WINS, BIG OR SMALL

When you make decisions that align with your true self, no matter how small, celebrate them. The more you acknowledge your own success in following your own path, the less power others' opinions will have. This can be as simple as taking a moment to congratulate yourself when you speak up for yourself or make a bold choice that others may not agree with.

Journaling Prompt: "What is one recent decision I made that I'm proud of, regardless of what others may have thought?"

6. EXERCISE: PRACTICE SILENCE AND OBSERVATION

Sometimes, we internalize the opinions of others without realizing it. Take a step back and observe your thoughts when you're around others, particularly in social settings or on social media. Do you find yourself changing your behavior or opinions to fit in? Practice silence in moments like these—don't feel the need to respond or adjust your stance. Just sit with your thoughts and notice how your body and mind feel without the pressure of external influence.

Journaling Prompt: "When do I feel the strongest need to adapt to others' opinions? How can I reclaim my own voice in these situations?"

7. EXERCISE: SURROUND YOURSELF WITH ENCOURAGING INFLUENCES

While it's important to ignore negative influences, it's just as important to surround yourself with people who lift you up and support your decisions. Make a list of people or environments that encourage you to be your authentic self, and spend more time with them. The more you immerse yourself in positive influences, the less you'll be swayed by negative opinions.

Journaling Prompt: "Who are the people that genuinely support my decisions? How can I nurture these relationships?"

8. EXERCISE: AFFIRMATIONS OF SELF-WORTH

Affirmations are a powerful tool to reinforce your sense of self-worth and detach from the opinions of others. Write down affirmations that remind you of your value, such as "I trust my judgment," "I am enough as I am," or "I am free to make choices based on what feels right to me." Recite these affirmations daily to strengthen your inner belief.

Journaling Prompt: "What affirmation will remind me that I am worthy of living my life based on my own values, not others' expectations?"

9. EXERCISE: VISUALIZE A LIFE FREE FROM EXTERNAL JUDGMENT

Take a few minutes each day to imagine a life where you're no longer affected by the opinions of others. Visualize yourself making decisions freely, feeling empowered, and living authentically without hesitation or fear. What does this life look like for you? What choices would you make if you were truly free from judgment?

Journaling Prompt: "What does my life look like when I stop letting others' opinions control my actions?"

10. EXERCISE: SHIFT FOCUS TO INTERNAL VALIDATION

Instead of seeking validation from others, practice giving yourself credit for the work you're doing and the choices you're making. Whether it's a career decision, a personal relationship, or a creative endeavor, acknowledge the steps you've taken to move toward your goals and the growth you've experienced along the way.

Journaling Prompt: "How can I celebrate my achievements without needing external validation?"

By practicing these exercises and journaling prompts, you can begin to shift your mindset from one that is dependent on others' opinions to one that is rooted in self-trust and authenticity. Each time you apply these steps, you'll reinforce your ability to break free from the grip of external judgments and take control of your life with confidence. Remember, your worth is not determined by others—it is defined by you. Keep embracing the power of "Let Them Be," and let your peace, freedom, and confidence grow.

HANDLING CRITICISM WITHOUT
LOSING CONFIDENCE

Depending on how we respond to it, handling criticism is one of those life skills that may either make us stronger or weaker. Since everyone appears to have an opinion, it's critical to learn how to take constructive criticism without allowing it to undermine your confidence or sense of self-worth. This is a process of developing your ability to filter out irrelevant remarks that don't merit your time and effort while simultaneously learning how to discern what is actually helpful. Let's examine how you may handle criticism and learn from it while maintaining your tranquility, independence, and self-assurance.

You may receive criticism from your family, friends, coworkers, or even complete strangers on social media. Sometimes it's helpful and intended to help you get better, and other times it's just a reflection of someone else's attitude, aggravation, or foolish attempt to feel better than them. The secret to prospering in an opinion-rich environment is to be able to tell the difference between the two and know how to deal with both without letting either determine your worth.

Refraining from taking criticism personally is the first step in dealing with it. It's simple to think that someone is attacking you personally when they criticize your work, choices, or personality. In actuality, though, all they are providing is their viewpoint on a particular conduct or deed. This is the point at which Mel Robbins' "Let Them Be" philosophy is applicable. People will have opinions; it doesn't matter if they are useful or valid. You don't have to internalize them just because they are permitted to express them. Their opinion doesn't define your identity or the worth of your work. You are greater than what other people think of you.

It's simpler to determine if criticism is beneficial or detrimental once you detach your identity from it. The goal of constructive criticism is to help you improve by concentrating on the behaviors or actions you can alter. Conversely, unhelpful criticism is not intended to assist you and frequently comes out as an assault on your abilities or character. Understanding the distinction is essential. Constructive criticism is usually actionable, detailed, and provided by someone who genuinely wants you to succeed. Despite the initial discomfort, this type of criticism offers a chance for development. Unlike helpful criticism, unhelpful criticism is about the other person and often feels harsh or ambiguous. You won't take it personally once you realize that.

Pausing to take a deep breath before responding is one of the most effective ways to deal with criticism. When someone points out something you've done incorrectly, it's normal to feel defensive, but acting rashly can make things worse. Instead, practice pausing to collect your thoughts, taking a deep breath, and then answering in a composed manner. While regaining control, you can consider how to respond to criticism.

Asking questions can also be beneficial during this period. Ask for details if the critique appears ambiguous or unjustified. For instance, ask, "Can you give me an example of what you mean?" rather than defending yourself. or "What should I do differently the next time, in your opinion?" By asking these questions, the discussion becomes fruitful rather than confrontational. They demonstrate your willingness to learn as well as your appreciation for lucidity and fruitful discussion.

You have the chance to use constructive criticism to further your own development. Consider what you can learn rather than how you feel. "What is the value in this feedback?" ask yourself. How can I get better with this knowledge? By doing this, you give yourself the ability to take charge of your own development instead of allowing the opinions of others to undermine your self-esteem.

However, it's crucial to establish limits with those who frequently provide unfavorable or unhelpful feedback. You need to learn how to let others "be" and cease letting them control your feelings or behavior, as Mel Robbins instructs. Even though you can't control others' actions, you can control your response. Setting a barrier is acceptable if someone is constantly criticizing without providing helpful criticism. You don't have to agree with every viewpoint that is expressed to you. One of the best ways to maintain your peace is to politely acknowledge someone else's viewpoint and then move on.

Self-reflection is the next tactic. When someone criticizes you, consider whether there is any truth or value in it. Consider asking yourself, "Is there anything I can do better?" or "Is there anything I can learn from this feedback?" Even when criticism seems harsh, it frequently contains a kernel of truth that might aid in your own development. If after some thought, the criticism doesn't support your beliefs or goals, ignore it. As you base your decisions on what you know to be true, reflection helps you grow from criticism and boosts confidence.

To handle criticism without losing your confidence, you must engage in self-compassion exercises in addition to reflection. None of us are flawless, and we all make mistakes. Instead of becoming overwhelmed by feelings of guilt or self-doubt when someone criticizes you, remind yourself that mistakes are a natural part of being human. An error or criticism does not define you or diminish your worth. Show yourself the same consideration and compassion that you would show a friend going through a similar situation.

Reminding yourself of your accomplishments and strengths will help you feel more confident. Make it a practice to enumerate your accomplishments, attributes, and all the things you've done right whenever you receive criticism. This can help you stay grounded and remind yourself that no one person's view can diminish your value or potential. It's about maintaining your identity in spite of what other people may think.

Keeping perspective is another crucial tactic. It's simple to become unduly fixated on someone else's viewpoint when you receive criticism, especially if that person's opinion is important to you. But in actuality, everyone has a unique viewpoint, and the truth of the matter is not defined by the critique of one individual. It is vital to keep in mind that criticism, especially from somebody you like or appreciate, is only one piece of information. You are complex, and one criticism does not capture your essence or abilities.

Lastly, never forget that criticism is a chance to make a decision. How much weight you give it and how you let it influence you are up to you. If necessary, you can ignore, use, or ask for clarification. However, you decide how to respond, and others' opinions don't have to lower your confidence. You'll become less affected by criticism and more rooted in your own worth and purpose as you keep using these techniques and implementing the Let Them Principle in your life.

Managing criticism is a talent that requires practice and time, just like any other ability. You will grow more assured of your capacity to take criticism without letting it diminish your sense of value the more you use these techniques. The objective is to learn how to filter criticism, grow from the positive aspects, and discard the things that don't help you, not to completely cease getting it. In addition to gaining self-assurance, doing this will help you feel more at ease and liberated when interacting with other people.

PRACTICAL EXERCISES

To help you handle criticism without losing confidence, applying the Let Them Principle is key. These practical exercises, examples, and journaling prompts will guide you in embracing criticism as a tool for growth while maintaining your self-assurance.

1. EXERCISE: SEPARATE CRITICISM FROM YOUR IDENTITY

When you receive criticism, pause before reacting. Ask yourself, "Is this feedback about my work/behavior, or is it about me as a person?" Write down how you feel in response to the criticism and then reflect on whether it's directed at your actions or your core identity. Practice reminding yourself that people can critique your actions, but they cannot touch your worth.

Journaling Prompt: Write about a time you received criticism. Did you internalize it? How did you separate it from your self-worth?

2. EXERCISE: THE PAUSE AND BREATHE TECHNIQUE

Next time you face criticism, take a deep breath before responding. This allows you time to process the feedback and maintain control over your reaction. After breathing, decide how to respond thoughtfully.

Example: You're at work and a colleague critiques your presentation. Instead of reacting immediately, take a moment to breathe, then ask, "Can you share one specific thing I can improve on?"

Journaling Prompt: Reflect on a situation where you reacted impulsively to criticism. How could you have handled it differently using the pause and breathe technique?

3. EXERCISE: IDENTIFY CONSTRUCTIVE VS. UNHELPFUL CRITICISM

Distinguish between criticism that can help you improve and criticism that is based on personal judgment. Constructive criticism is specific and actionable, while unhelpful criticism tends to be vague or unnecessarily harsh.

Journaling Prompt: Think of a recent piece of criticism you received. Was it constructive or unhelpful? How did it affect you? What did you learn from it, if anything?

4. EXERCISE: PRACTICE SELF-AFFIRMATION AFTER CRITICISM

After receiving feedback, especially if it's tough to hear, affirm your value. Write three things about yourself that you are proud of, regardless of the feedback you've received. This can be achievements, qualities, or ways you've contributed positively.

Example: After a tough meeting where your idea was criticized, remind yourself, "I am capable," "I've had success in the past," and "I can learn and grow from this feedback."

Journaling Prompt: Write down three affirmations about your skills or qualities. How does reminding yourself of your strengths help you move past criticism?

5. EXERCISE: REFRAME NEGATIVE FEEDBACK

Take a piece of criticism you didn't like and reframe it in a way that is more empowering. If someone says your work "isn't good enough," reframe it as, "This feedback is an opportunity to improve and push my skills further."

Journaling Prompt: Reframe a piece of recent criticism in a way that empowers you. How does this new perspective change your view of the feedback?

6. EXERCISE: SET HEALTHY BOUNDARIES AROUND UNHELPFUL CRITICISM

If someone repeatedly offers criticism that is not constructive, practice saying no and setting boundaries. Politely but firmly tell them, "I understand your opinion, but I prefer to focus on solutions."

Example: If a friend or colleague constantly criticizes your personal choices, calmly say, "I appreciate that you care, but I prefer to make my own decisions. Let's talk about something else."

Journaling Prompt: Have you had to set boundaries with someone offering excessive criticism? How did you do it, and how did it make you feel?

7. EXERCISE: FIND THE LESSON IN EVERY CRITICISM

Ask yourself what you can learn from each piece of criticism, even if it stings at first. Can it help you improve? Can you use it to refine your approach or skills?

Example: If your boss criticizes a report you submitted, ask yourself, "What specific feedback can I use to make my next report better?"

Journaling Prompt: Write about a recent criticism and reflect on the lessons you learned from it. How can this help you grow?

8. EXERCISE: SELF-COMPASSION AFTER CRITICISM

After receiving criticism, practice self-compassion. Remind yourself that everyone makes mistakes and no one is perfect. Give yourself permission to be human and not perfect.

Example: If your performance at work wasn't up to standard, instead of berating yourself, say, "I gave my best effort, and I can learn from this."

Journaling Prompt: When you make a mistake or receive criticism, how do you treat yourself? Write about a time you showed yourself compassion after criticism.

9. EXERCISE: REVISIT PAST SUCCESSES

Whenever you face criticism, take a moment to revisit your past achievements. This reminds you of your capabilities and serves as a counterbalance to negative feedback.

Example: When you're feeling down after a tough critique, write down 5 accomplishments that make you proud and remind yourself of your growth.

Journaling Prompt: Write down five things you've achieved that make you proud. How can you draw strength from these accomplishments when receiving criticism?

By incorporating these exercises into your routine, you can develop a more grounded and confident approach to handling criticism. You'll start to see it as a tool for growth rather than something that threatens your worth. The Let Them Principle empowers you to filter through the noise of others' opinions and focus on what truly matters. You get to choose which feedback is useful, and which you can let go of, all while maintaining your peace, freedom, and confidence.

FINDING JOY IN LETTING GO

We frequently become caught up in a loop of planning, striving, and clinging to control in life. We think that everything will turn out the way we want it to if we just hang on a bit longer. However, the truth is that this demand for control frequently leads to more stress than it relieves. It drains us and keeps us in a state of perpetual anxiety. The more we attempt to control the path, the more we oppose life's organic flow. And we lose the capacity for joy in that opposition.

Inspired by Mel Robbins' teachings, the Let Them Principle encourages us to let go of our need for control and accept things as they are. This process of letting go is about realizing what we can and cannot manage; it's not about letting go or escaping responsibilities. We give ourselves access to freedom, happiness, and serenity when we learn to distinguish between the two and concentrate on the things we can actually affect.

Consider the case of Sarah, a lady who attempted to manage every element of her life for years. Sarah felt the urge to control all aspects of her life, including her relationships and profession. She made sure everything was flawless, scheduled every hour of the day, and attempted to address issues before they even came up. But something was always wrong, no matter how hard she tried. She was always anxious and worried about what could go wrong. Every day seemed to elude her happiness more and more.

Sarah decided to try something new one day after having yet another breakdown over something that hadn't gone as planned. She started playing around with the concept of letting go—letting go of her strict routines, her desire for control, and her dread of the future. She began to watch and accept life as it was, rather than imposing her plans on it. She allowed herself to feel disappointed when a meeting didn't go as planned, but she refrained from becoming angry. She stopped taking a friend's cancellation of plans as a personal rejection and just moved on. Sarah began to feel lighter gradually as she let go of the urge to be in charge of everything.

Although it took some time for this change to occur, Sarah gradually started to feel more free. She was no longer bound by the results of every circumstance. She discovered that life went more smoothly when she relinquished control. Moments of unanticipated happiness also accompanied that flow, moments she may have missed if she had been too preoccupied with trying to make everything fit. Sarah started to feel tranquility in ways she had never experienced before; she eventually came to accept life's unpredictable nature. This tale emphasizes a vital reality: accepting life's ups and downs is what it means to let go, not to be passive. It's about accepting accountability for the things under your control and letting go of the rest. Joy is pushed away the more you cling to control. The more we resist, the more we struggle against our own happiness because life has a way of surprising us.

It's not always simple to let go. It calls for a readiness to believe that things don't have to go as planned. Although giving up is first uncomfortable, the freedom and serenity that result are worth it. It involves making the decision to not let your internal state be dictated by the situations outside of you. You may be more present, more adaptable, and ultimately happier when you let go of the urge for control, whether it's during a challenging conversation, a career transition, or an unforeseen setback.

Mel Robbins discusses how our brains are programmed to take charge and avoid discomfort in his book *The 5-Second Rule*. However, we may start rewiring our brains and overcoming the need to control everything by employing the 5-second rule to overcome that initial resistance. In terms of letting go, this is recognizing when you are tempted to micromanage or fixate on the result and using those five seconds to change your viewpoint. Think about how you could use this in your own life. It's possible that you feel compelled to regulate your partner's activities or behaviors in your relationship. You may be under continual pressure to have everything worked out because of your career, yet this pressure only makes you feel uncomfortable and unhappy. Perhaps it's just the usual annoyances of life, like traffic, doing errands, or juggling other people's schedules. These situations all present chances to practice letting go.

The room it makes for joy is one of the most potent effects of letting go of control. The moment you stop worrying about how things should be, you experience them. Whether it's a peaceful cup of coffee in the morning, a moment of laughter with friends, or the fulfillment of a project well done without all the strain you've put on it, you find the beauty in the little things.

We miss these times when we were obsessed with controlling everything, even if they were always there.

Allowing ourselves to be human is another aspect of letting go. It's acceptable to not know everything or to watch events unfold without understanding every detail. It is thrilling to realize the freedom that follows. You no longer feel constrained by other people's opinions or by your own expectations. You discover tranquility when you accept life as it is.

Understanding that control is a myth is one of the most crucial parts of letting go. Even though we may believe we are in control, all we really control over is how we react to the events of life. The result is frequently out of our grasp. This insight can be uplifting as well as humbling. It relieves us of the burden of attempting to foresee and manage every situation, enabling us to concentrate on what really matters: how we behave in the world, how we treat people and ourselves, and how we accept life as it comes.

The joy of letting go comes from trusting that everything will be okay. We can't always predict how life will turn out, but when we let go of our need to be in charge, we allow ourselves to be receptive to whatever happens. And we discover joy, freedom, and peace in that openness.

It's a drastic change in viewpoint. It's about choosing to concentrate on the things we can control, including our thoughts, our actions, and our reactions, rather than avoiding responsibility. The more we nurture joy, the more we practice this. We start to appreciate life's inherent beauty in all its unpredictable ways as we let go of the impulse to push things.

Ultimately, embracing life's obstacles with openness and acceptance rather than accepting them is what makes letting go enjoyable. We make room for the unanticipated pleasures that life has to offer when we let go of our goals and expectations. The secret is to have faith that we may be content without having complete control over our lives. And in that trust, we find the freedom and tranquility we've long sought. Let go and let life unfold in all of its messy, gorgeous splendor.

PRACTICAL EXERCISES

EXERCISE 1: LETTING GO OF CONTROL IN SMALL MOMENTS

Start by identifying one area of your life where you try to control things. It could be your daily routine, a relationship, or how you manage work tasks. For one day, consciously choose to let go of control in that area. Instead of stressing about outcomes, let things unfold naturally. Notice how it feels. Do you experience relief or frustration? Keep track of your feelings and write them down.

Example: If you usually plan your entire workday hour by hour, choose to leave some parts unplanned and let them flow as they come. Observe how it affects your energy levels and mood.

JOURNALING PROMPT 1: THE BURDEN OF CONTROL

Think about a recent situation where you tried to control the outcome of something or someone. How did it make you feel? Did it bring you peace, or did it increase your anxiety? Write about how you could have handled it differently by releasing control, and imagine how it could have turned out if you had chosen to let go.

EXERCISE 2: SURRENDERING TO THE FLOW

This exercise focuses on the process of releasing attachment to specific outcomes. Choose a task you typically try to control. For example, if you're working on a project, let go of perfectionism and give yourself permission to simply do your best without obsessing over every detail. Focus on the experience, not the result. Afterward, reflect on how you felt when you let go of the pressure.

Example: If you're painting or cooking, allow yourself to experiment without worrying about the end product. See how this affects the quality of the experience and your emotional state.

JOURNALING PROMPT 2: RELEASING EXPECTATIONS

Write about a time when you let go of expectations and felt liberated. What happened when you allowed things to unfold naturally instead of forcing them? How did you feel afterward? Did you notice any change in your emotional state, such as relief or happiness? Reflect on what you learned about yourself through this process.

EXERCISE 3: CELEBRATING IMPERFECTION

Release the need for everything to be perfect. Each day, choose one thing you usually try to perfect and let it be imperfect. It might be something small, like leaving your home a bit messy or letting a conversation happen without overthinking it. Celebrate the freedom that comes with embracing imperfection.

Example: Instead of worrying about getting every email just right, send it without over-editing. Allow yourself to feel proud of moving forward instead of getting stuck in perfectionism.

JOURNALING PROMPT 3: THE JOY OF IMPERFECTION

Think of a moment in the past week where you embraced imperfection. Write about how it felt to let go of the need to be perfect. Were you surprised by the joy or relief it brought? What did you learn from this experience?

EXERCISE 4: LETTING GO OF JUDGMENTS

Write down a situation where you felt judgment toward yourself or others. Reflect on why you felt the need to judge. Now, practice letting go of that judgment. Release the urge to control or critique the situation. Instead, focus on acceptance, understanding, or simply observing without reacting.

Example: If you judged someone for being late, try to let go of that judgment and focus on accepting the situation for what it is.

JOURNALING PROMPT 4: THE FREEDOM OF NON-JUDGMENT

Reflect on a moment in your life when you felt free from judgment, whether toward yourself or others. Write about how that freedom felt. How did your mind and body react when you didn't judge or control the situation? What did it teach you about yourself and your relationships?

EXERCISE 5: PRACTICING TRUST

Pick one area of your life where you often feel the need to control, such as your career or a relationship. Write down your fears related to letting go of control in this area. Then, identify one small action you can take to trust the process instead of controlling it. This might be allowing someone else to lead in a conversation or giving up a task at work. Take that action and observe the results.

Example: If you often worry about your job performance, try delegating a small task to someone else and trust that they will do it well.

JOURNALING PROMPT 5: BUILDING TRUST IN THE UNKNOWN

Write about an area of your life where you struggle to trust the process. What makes it difficult for you to let go of control? Explore your emotions and fears surrounding this situation. How would releasing control in this area bring more joy and freedom into your life? What could you learn from trusting in the unknown?

EXERCISE 6: RELEASING PEOPLE-PLEASING

If you tend to worry about others' opinions or try to please everyone around you, take a moment to reflect on how this affects your joy. Choose one situation where you normally people-please, and practice letting go of the need for approval. Instead, focus on what feels right for you.

Example: Instead of over-apologizing for something you didn't do wrong, allow yourself to simply stand firm in your truth.

JOURNALING PROMPT 6: SAYING NO TO PEOPLE-PLEASING

Think of a time when you said "yes" to something out of fear of disappointing others. How did it make you feel? Write about the impact of letting go of people-pleasing tendencies. How can you practice releasing this habit in a healthy way, and what benefits would that bring to your peace and joy?

EXERCISE 7: RELEASING THE PAST

Think about something from your past that you're still holding onto, whether it's a mistake you made or something that someone did to you. Write about how this past experience continues to affect your present. Now, practice releasing it. Write a letter to your past self or the person involved, expressing forgiveness or understanding. Afterward, let go of any attachment to that experience and move forward.

Example: If you're still holding onto anger from a past conflict, write a letter that acknowledges the hurt, but also let go of the need to carry that pain forward.

JOURNALING PROMPT 7: LETTING GO OF THE PAST

What is something from your past that you're still holding onto? Reflect on how it's affecting your current life and relationships. Write about the process of letting go of this past burden. How would your life change if you truly released it? What would you be able to embrace or enjoy once you do?

These exercises and journaling prompts are designed to help you gradually apply the Let Them Principle to your daily life, allowing you to experience the freedom, peace, and joy that come with letting go of control, judgments, and the need to please others. By incorporating these practices, you'll begin to notice how much lighter and more confident you feel as you release the things that no longer serve you.

CHAPTER 4

Building Unshakable Confidence

THE CONNECTION BETWEEN
CONTROL AND SELF-DOUBT

The desire to control everything in our lives can often be traced back to one key feeling: self-doubt. We attempt to control the environment around us in an attempt to provide consistency, comfort, and reassurance when we don't feel safe in ourselves. Although this urge for control is a protective mechanism, it may also be a trap that hinders our development and feeds self-doubt. We unconsciously acknowledge that we don't trust ourselves or the environment around us the more we cling to control. However, relinquishing power boosts confidence.

One of the most surprising lessons of giving up control is that we don't know everything. We may trust ourselves to adapt and change even when we make decisions without knowing the precise result. We let go of strict plans and allow life to unfold naturally. By doing this, we break free from the pattern of doubting and second-guessing our decisions, which only makes them worse. Attempting to manage everything makes us think about "what ifs." Uncertainty paralyzes us, causing us to doubt the wisdom of our choices, worry if we're doing enough, and fear failure. Our fears are exacerbated the more we want to exercise control. We seem to be one mistake away from proving our inadequacy and one step away from catastrophe. Control comes from fear, which comes from self-doubt.

Consider someone who is constantly concerned with what other people think of them. Because they are afraid of being judged, they carefully consider everything they say and do, and they are always looking for acceptance. They become more nervous as they try to control others' opinions. Ironically, this attempt to influence other people's opinions simply serves to increase their self-doubt. Our self-doubt would start to fade if we could just let go of the desire to dictate what other people think of us. We would discover that we are sufficient just the way we are.

Understanding that failure is a necessary element of growth and not something to be feared is one of the most transformative effects of relinquishing control. The delusion that everything must be flawless is a breeding ground for self-doubt. By letting go of that delusion and acknowledging that errors are unavoidable, we allow ourselves to grow from them instead of punishing ourselves for them. You stop pushing yourself to unreasonable expectations when you let go of the impulse to control every outcome. You let go of the worry that making mistakes will make you appear incompetent or undeserving.

Think about someone starting a new company. They may experience intense pressure to make sure every little thing is ideal, including every marketing plan and client encounter. Due to fear of failure, they micromanage the entire company, which makes them doubt themselves. "What if this fails?" they ask themselves. What if this isn't my calling? The burden, however, relieves when they decide to relinquish control over every aspect and give themselves permission to make mistakes. Knowing that they are capable of handling any situation, they start acting without fear of failure.

In addition, giving up control teaches us to trust the process, even if it fails. Giving up control—not of other people or circumstances, but of yourself—requires a certain amount of faith. We become more confident when we have faith in our ability to change, modify, and deal with obstacles as they come along. The belief that we are unable to manage the uncertainty is the foundation of self-doubt. However, as we let go, we realize that the unknown is not a threat but rather a chance for development.

Letting go necessitates vulnerability. We put ourselves in danger of not knowing what will happen next. However, we let our genuine confidence show through when we are vulnerable. Being confident is having faith in our abilities regardless of the circumstances, not having all the answers, or being in charge. It's about maintaining our identity in the face of uncertainty. Letting go gives us a strong message that we don't need to micromanage every aspect of our lives and that we are sufficient just the way we are.

Relationships could serve as an illustration of this. Fear frequently drives our attempts to exert control over others, whether it be through forcing a particular result or altering a partner's behavior. We may be afraid of being rejected, of being left alone, or of losing control of the circumstance. This attempt at control leads to conflict and uncertainty. However, when we let go, we don't strive to shape the relationship into a certain shape; instead, we let it grow organically. We have faith that everyone will be true to themselves, and whatever occurs will happen. This eases the tension and makes it possible to connect authentically, which increases trust and boosts relationship confidence.

Giving up the need for perfection is another aspect of letting go. We frequently aim for perfection in all facets of our lives—our relationships, our careers, our appearances, and even our thoughts—in our quest for control. The urge to manage every aspect and be flawless simply serves to draw attention to our flaws and deepen our self-doubt. However, we cease evaluating ourselves according to impossible standards when we accept our imperfections. We begin to see that our worth is independent of flawless execution or ideal results. The belief that we are valuable, flaws and all, underpins confidence. Acceptance is a strong approach to overcoming self-doubt through letting go. When we accept that we cannot control everything, we can control our response. It is not the same as resignation. By letting go of the need to control, we believe that we can manage any situation that comes our way and accept ourselves and our circumstances as they are. As we begin to trust our own judgment and cease depending on outside affirmation, this acceptance strengthens our inner power.

One important tip is to start small. If you have a tendency to micromanage or overthink things, pick one aspect of your life to let go of control over and see what happens. Allowing a friend to select the plans for a night out rather than organizing everything yourself could be the answer. Or it can entail declining a project at work that is beyond your purview, despite your possible concern that it will reflect negatively on you. See how it changes your perspective when you begin to let go in tiny, doable steps. As you see that you can manage any situation without having to exert control, this practice will gradually boost your confidence.

Another tactic is to identify when self-doubt is at its height and consider whether you're attempting to exert control over something that is beyond your control. Are you preoccupied with other people's opinions? Are you worried about something over which you have no control? During these times, remind yourself that letting go of control is the first step toward freedom. Breathe deeply, resist the need to second-guess yourself, and have faith that you will be fine no matter what happens.

Lastly, one of the most significant insights is that confidence is a process rather than a final goal. It's learned by letting go, not by taking charge of everything. Your self-doubt will decrease as you work on letting go of control and accepting uncertainty. As you let go, you believe you can adapt and succeed no matter what. Letting go eventually develops into a habit that gives you the ability to deal with life's obstacles more easily and confidently.

LETTING GO OF PERFECTIONISM

Perfectionism frequently poses as a noble endeavor. We persuade ourselves that aiming for perfection in all facets of our lives will bring us fulfillment, success, and approval. However, perfectionism is actually a subtle kind of self-defeating behavior. It skews our expectations, increases stress, and inhibits development. The pressure to accomplish everything flawlessly can be overwhelming and harmful, even when the desire to do things properly is understandable. Perfectionism's strain is a burdensome burden. Perfectionism informs us that every error is a failure, that anything less than perfect is unacceptable, and that we should always aim for an impossible goal. Because we are continuously striving for an ideal that might not even exist, it causes tension. We deprive ourselves of freedom and tranquility when we push ourselves to impossible ideals.

What occurs when we strive for perfection? We give the appearance of control. When people dread uncertainty, perfectionism flourishes. We think that if everything were done perfectly, there would be peace at last. But life isn't like that. Life is unpredictable no matter how much we attempt to control the outcome. Furthermore, striving for perfection only makes life more tiring rather than more predictable. Every minor flaw turns into an indication of failure, and every error into an excuse for feeling unworthy. Our sense of success is diminished when we dwell on the things we didn't do well rather than the progress we've made.

Burnout results from the accumulation of this pressure over time. Rather than focusing on our strengths, perfectionism makes us overly conscious of our shortcomings. It skews our perception, causing us to concentrate primarily on the issues that require attention. We are unable to completely appreciate what is right because we are always focused on what is wrong. Despite the fact that mistakes are an unavoidable aspect of life, we interpret every setback as a sign that we are inadequate.

The paradox of perfectionism is that it frequently keeps us from acting at all. We do nothing because we're afraid of making mistakes. We remain inactive because we feel that everything must be flawless. Because we are so preoccupied with avoiding mistakes, we overthink, overanalyze, and overplan, but we never take the initial move. Perfectionism paralyzes us rather than fostering advancement. It prevents us from ever attempting in an effort to prevent us from failing.

Accepting imperfection is the cure to this strain. We give ourselves permission to be human when we let go of the pressure to accomplish everything flawlessly. We acknowledge that learning is a continuous process and that mistakes are inevitable. Admitting we don't have to be perfect to succeed is embracing imperfection, not mediocrity. It entails realizing that learning occurs by experience, stepping outside of our comfort zones, and having the courage to fail.

We may act without the paralyzing dread of making mistakes when we let go of our perfectionism. It lets us experiment without having to worry about doing things perfectly. We provide ourselves permission to proceed when we acknowledge that imperfections are a natural part of existence. We start taking flawed action immediately and stop waiting for the perfect time to start. Knowing that every step—even the mistakes—is a part of the process, we stop waiting for the ideal circumstances and begin working with what we have. We also start to let go of the need for outside approval when we accept our imperfections. Perfectionism frequently flourishes based on other people's perceptions. Whether it's in our relationships, our jobs, or our looks, we want to seem perfect to others around us. However, we release ourselves from the ongoing pressure to live up to others' expectations when we let go of this urge. We no longer base our value on other people's opinions. We begin to define success according to our own principles rather than an impossible ideal.

This change in viewpoint creates a whole new range of opportunities. We are free to be ourselves without being pressured by the never-ending quest for perfection. We start to value our individuality and flaws, realizing that they define us as human. We come to see that our imperfections enhance our resilience, relatability, and authenticity rather than diminishing our worth. We develop, learn, and change as a result of our flaws.

It takes time for this mentality to change. Consciously letting up on perfectionism is necessary. It calls on us to deliberately pick a new course of action when we start to think in a perfectionistic manner. We must allow ourselves the freedom to fail, make mistakes, and try again. It entails trusting our own judgment and letting go of the need for other people's acceptance. It entails honoring the procedure as well as the final product.

Learning to question the assumptions that underpin perfectionism is a crucial step in this process. What am I terrified of, and why do I feel the need to be flawless? Perfectionism frequently stems from fear—fear of not being good enough, fear of failing, and fear of being judged. However, perfectionism exacerbates these anxieties rather than allays them. We may let go of the impulse to avoid fear at all costs when we acknowledge that it is a normal aspect of life. We learn to confront fear and failure head-on and keep going forward, rather than trying to manage everything to avoid them.

Realizing that our value is independent of our accomplishments is among the most freeing insights that result from letting go of perfectionism. To be valuable, we don't have to be flawless. To be successful, liked, and respected, we don't have to be perfect. We are valuable for who we are, not for how perfect we appear to others. This insight enables us to just present ourselves as who we truly are, releasing the pressure to be flawless.

Self-compassion is also necessary for letting go of perfectionism. As we make mistakes, we must be kind to ourselves and accept that our efforts are enough. Embracing imperfection teaches us to treat ourselves with compassion and empathy, yet perfectionism frequently involves harsh self-criticism. Instead of condemning ourselves for every error, we should celebrate the bravery required to attempt new things and take chances.

Accepting flaws is a life-changing experience. It makes room for individual development, inventiveness, and originality. We begin to perceive new opportunities and solutions when we lose our obsession with perfection. We give ourselves permission to think creatively and take chances that we might not have otherwise taken because we are afraid of failing. We get more flexible, adaptive, and eager to take on tasks that previously seemed too difficult. When we embrace progress and cease striving for perfection, growth occurs.

When we accept our imperfections, we begin to view errors as teaching moments rather than as failures. We understand that there are many obstacles and detours on the path to success; it is not a straight line. However, every stride—no matter how faulty—brings us one step closer to our goal. Letting up on perfectionism allows us to see the limitless potential that comes with imperfection and relieves us of the weight of unattainable expectations. True growth takes place in this area of imperfection.

With an emphasis on letting go of perfectionism, the following useful activities, examples, and writing prompts will assist you in implementing the Let Them Principle in your everyday life:

EXERCISE 1: IDENTIFY YOUR PERFECTIONIST TRIGGERS

Goal: To become aware of when perfectionism is taking hold and consciously choose to let go.

Instructions:

1. Take a moment each day to reflect on any areas of your life where you feel the need to be perfect. Write down what triggered this feeling.

2. Think about the last time you felt paralyzed by perfectionism. What was the outcome? Did you get closer to your goal, or did you avoid taking action?

3. Write a list of alternative ways to approach these situations without striving for perfection. What would be "good enough" to move forward?

Example:

You may realize that you put off sending emails at work because you're obsessing over the wording. Instead of perfection, challenge yourself to send the email after a set amount of time, trusting that it's clear enough without overthinking.

EXERCISE 2: IMPERFECT ACTION CHALLENGE

Goal: To build comfort with imperfection and stop overanalyzing every step.

Instructions:

1. Choose one task you've been avoiding because you feel it needs to be done perfectly.

2. Set a timer for 15 minutes and begin working on it without any expectation of completing it perfectly. The only rule is that you must stop after the timer goes off, regardless of the outcome.

3. Reflect on how it felt to release control. Did it open up more creativity? Did you feel more accomplished by moving forward despite not reaching perfection?

Example:

If you've been avoiding working on a presentation because you think it has to be flawless, try drafting a few slides without worrying about the design or wording. By the end of the timer, you'll have made progress rather than staying stuck.

EXERCISE 3: CELEBRATE IMPERFECT MOMENTS

Goal: To shift your mindset and find joy in the process instead of perfection.

Instructions:

1. Each day, write down one moment where you let go of perfectionism. This can be small, like making a decision without second-guessing yourself or allowing a small mistake to slide.

2. Give yourself credit for showing up and trying. Acknowledge that mistakes are part of your growth, not a sign of failure.

Example:

You might celebrate allowing your house to stay messy for a while so you could enjoy quality time with your family, or perhaps you submitted a project with minor imperfections instead of spending extra hours getting it "just right."

JOURNALING PROMPTS:

1. "What would it feel like to do this task imperfectly and let go of the pressure?"

This prompt encourages self-reflection on the feelings that perfectionism brings up and helps you release them. It allows you to imagine freedom from perfectionism, even if only for a moment.

2. "When was the last time I feared judgment for being imperfect? What did I learn from that experience?"

Reflect on times you allowed perfectionism to dictate your actions out of fear of judgment. What insights have you gained from those experiences? How can you choose to embrace imperfection in the future?

3. "What would I tell a friend who is struggling with perfectionism?"

Sometimes, we are kinder to others than to ourselves. By journaling as if you're giving advice to someone you care about, you may discover how to treat yourself with more compassion.

4. "What is one thing I can do today to take imperfect action toward a goal?"

Challenge yourself to take one small step toward a goal, no matter how messy or imperfect the process may feel. This can help dissolve the need to be perfect and increase momentum.

Example Scenario:

Imagine you're working on a personal project, and the task seems daunting because you believe it needs to be flawless. You decide to start by writing down your ideas without worrying about structure or grammar, giving yourself permission to be imperfect. The action of writing itself becomes more important than crafting something perfect. By focusing on moving forward, you remove the paralysis perfectionism often brings.

EXERCISE 4: RELEASE THE COMPARISON TRAP

Goal: To focus on your progress without comparing yourself to others.

Instructions:

1. Identify one area where you often compare yourself to others, whether it's at work, in your personal life, or on social media.

2. Acknowledge how this comparison is rooted in perfectionism and how it makes you feel.

3. Instead of comparing, make a list of your unique strengths and successes. Write about the things that make you proud of who you are.

Example:

If you often compare your career progress to a colleague's, remind yourself of your unique path and the milestones you've reached. Celebrate where you are instead of wishing you were further along.

By incorporating these exercises, examples, and journaling prompts into your daily life, you can begin to loosen the grip of perfectionism. Embrace the idea that progress, not perfection, leads to true growth. With each small act of letting go, you create more space for peace, freedom, and confidence. The Let Them Principle invites you to stop holding yourself hostage to perfection, giving you the power to show up in your life as you are—imperfect, yet whole.

EMBRACING AUTHENTICITY

A freeing sensation that many people desire yet frequently find difficult to attain is living genuinely. The demands of society and the views of people around us ensnare us. Our sense of self may be distorted by these influences, causing us to become someone we believe other people want us to be instead of who we really are. By embracing authenticity, you may let go of the layers of outside approval and present yourself as complete, unadulterated, and authentic. It's about having the guts to step into the person you were always intended to be and let go of the roles you've been taught to play.

It takes time to go through this process of honesty. It calls for a dedication to self-awareness, self-acceptance, and a readiness to let go of the desire for other people's approval. The opinions and expectations of others ensnare a significant deal of our sense of self-worth. We are socialized from an early age to conform—to live up to expectations regarding our achievements, conduct, or looks. We are frequently encouraged to place more importance on outward recognition than on inner fulfillment. We become more disconnected from ourselves as we seek outside approval.

The Let Them Principle urges us to cease constantly seeking acceptance from others and to let go of the need to manage how they see us. We can make room to develop a better awareness of ourselves by letting go of these expectations. It's about making the decision to live your life on your own terms rather than following someone else's plan. However, we must first determine the factors that are preventing us from breaking free from the cycle of seeking approval. In particular, our societal norms create a high standard for achievement, happiness, and success. We are encouraged to compete, to constantly aim higher, and to achieve success in ways that are quantifiable and apparent. This results in a feeling of self-worth that is determined more by accomplishments and outward looks than by inborn traits like generosity, kindness, or genuineness. Inspired by Mel Robbins' teachings, the Let Them Principle presents an alternative viewpoint that enables us to trust ourselves rather than join the herd and resist social pressure.

Letting go of the idea that we need to live up to other people's expectations in order to be valued is the foundation of embracing authenticity. We become closer to living genuinely every time we choose to live in accordance with our actual desires rather than fitting into the roles that others have assigned us. For instance, deciding to voice your thoughts in social or professional contexts, even when they don't align with the group's consensus, can be a potent act of self-empowerment. Realizing that you don't need to justify yourself to others is equally crucial. Insecurity or a fear of being judged are common causes of the desire to defend our decisions. You give yourself the freedom to behave in ways that are authentically you when you break this habit.

You trust your own judgment and conclusions when you stop caring what others think. The process of gaining confidence is slow. You strengthen the idea that you are sufficient just the way you are the more you practice being real. However, this can be unsettling, particularly at first. When you attempt to break free from habits that have protected you for a long time, even if those patterns are restrictive, it's normal to feel resistance. You must overcome your fear and discomfort in order to embrace authenticity and have faith that the benefits will greatly exceed your early suffering.

It's critical to recognize that being authentic does not entail living without empathy or compromise. It all comes down to striking a balance between taking care of yourself and those around you. You may remain loyal to yourself and still have positive connections and relationships. Being authentic is speaking and acting from a position of clarity and truth rather than being harsh or dismissing other people's viewpoints.

It can be immensely freeing to let go of the worry of being judged by others. Realizing others' opinions don't define you is a first step. For many reasons, people may reject or condemn you, but their fears and insecurities often cause these reactions. You can start to let go of the emotional weight these opinions have on you once you realize this. You can live more fully and confidently when you let go of the desire to manage how other people perceive you.

Self-compassion is also necessary for embracing honesty. We are frequently our own worst critics, and it may be quite challenging to quiet the voice inside of us that tells us we are inadequate. However, in order to live a genuine life, we need to learn to treat ourselves with the same consideration and compassion that we would show a friend. Self-compassion enables us to be authentic, flaws and all, without feeling the need to alter or conceal who we are in order to win acceptance. We emphasize what we have to offer in our purest form rather than what we lack.

Adopting honesty might occasionally feel like a rebellious move, particularly if you've spent years attempting to live up to social or romantic standards. Saying no to things that don't fit with your values or going against the grain in favor of a route that feels true to you can be awkward. But it takes guts to live truly, and the more you do it, the more it comes naturally. Eventually, the initial unease will give way to independence, serenity, and a greater sense of fulfillment.

Imagine how powerful it would be to wake up every day knowing that you are living for yourself and not for the approval of others. You can discover who you are and what brings you joy when you let go of others' expectations. You start focusing on your wants rather than your needs.

A compelling illustration of embracing authenticity is seen in the life of a person who felt constrained by social and professional expectations. To satisfy family expectations, they pretended to be someone they weren't and worked in a job they didn't enjoy for years. They chose to take a chance and seek a career that matched their enthusiasm after years of repressing their own wants. Although it wasn't an effortless move, they eventually discovered that their new route brought them more happiness, fulfillment, and pleasure. The choice to really live, unrestricted by social conventions and instead motivated by their own aspirations and interests, was the foundation of this change.

Letting up on unhealthy relationships that sap your energy or impede your progress is another aspect of living genuinely. Because it forces them out of their comfort zones, some won't support you fully. People who depend on you to be a certain way for their personal gain frequently exhibit this trait. Knowing these relationships for what they are may help you choose who you let into your life. Although ending these relationships may be difficult, doing so eventually gives you the opportunity to be with people who value your true selves.

Being real is a journey that lasts a lifetime. It calls for perseverance, awareness, and a readiness to deal with discomfort. However, if you follow the Let Them Principle, you'll discover how to let go of the need for approval from others and welcome the liberation that comes from living authentically. Step into a life that reflects your innermost wishes and release the false narratives and expectations that have imprisoned you. Greater serenity, self-assurance, and a sense of fulfillment that only comes from living will truly be yours as you proceed.

Ultimately, being genuine to oneself isn't the only aspect of authenticity. It's about designing a life that feels right for you since you've taken the time to figure out who you really are, not because other people think it should. After you've done that, you'll realize that you've only ever required your own approval.

Here are some useful activities, examples, and journaling prompts to assist you in embracing authenticity through the use of the Let Them Principle:

1. SELF-REFLECTION EXERCISE: IDENTIFYING YOUR TRUE SELF

- **Goal:** Get clear on who you are beneath societal expectations.
- **How:** Set aside 15 minutes each day to sit quietly and reflect. Write down the roles you play in life (e.g., daughter, employee, partner) and explore which of these feel authentic and which feel like you're performing to meet

expectations. Identify where you feel the most true to yourself and where you feel disconnected.

- **Example:** If you are a professional but feel stifled by your corporate role, consider what part of you is yearning to be expressed outside of that role (e.g., creativity, personal passions).

2. DAILY PRACTICE: SHOW UP AS YOU ARE

- **Goal:** Practice small acts of authenticity every day.
- **How:** Commit to one action each day that aligns with your true self, regardless of how others may perceive it. This could be as simple as speaking up in a meeting, wearing something that makes you feel confident, or expressing your opinion when you usually remain silent.
- **Example:** If you're in a social situation where you typically agree with others to avoid conflict, practice respectfully disagreeing and stating your own perspective. Notice how it feels to be true to yourself.

3. JOURNALING PROMPT: LETTING GO OF EXTERNAL APPROVAL

- **Goal:** Explore your relationship with external validation and identify how it impacts your authenticity.
- **Prompt:** Write about a recent situation where you felt the need for approval from others. How did it feel? What would have happened if you didn't seek their approval and simply followed your own instincts? How might that have changed the outcome?
- **Example:** You might write about a time you held back a personal opinion in a meeting to avoid rocking the boat. Reflect on how that made you feel and how things might have shifted if you spoke up.

4. EXERCISE: RELEASING THE NEED FOR PERFECTION

- **Goal:** Let go of perfectionism and embrace imperfection as part of your authentic self.
- **How:** For one week, take note of every time you find yourself striving for perfection in your appearance, work, or relationships. Each time, ask yourself: "Am I trying to meet someone else's standard, or is this what truly feels right for me?" Make a note of how you can allow yourself to be imperfect in each situation.
- **Example:** If you're preparing a meal for friends, instead of striving for a perfectly plated dish, allow yourself to embrace the imperfections—like a rustic presentation and focus on the experience of sharing the meal with them, not how "perfect" it looks.

5. JOURNALING PROMPT: REDEFINING SUCCESS ON YOUR TERMS

- **Goal:** Shift your perspective on success from external definitions to your own.
- **Prompt:** Write about what success looks like for you without considering anyone else's view. What brings you joy, fulfillment, and satisfaction, regardless of societal expectations or external pressures? How can you begin to incorporate these elements into your daily life?
- **Example:** If your career has been driven by external rewards like promotions or status, think about what success looks like if it's about personal satisfaction or work-life balance. How can you integrate these values into your day-to-day life?

6. PRACTICAL EXAMPLE: AUTHENTICITY IN RELATIONSHIPS

- **Goal:** Practice being authentically yourself in your relationships.
- **How:** Take an honest look at your closest relationships. Are you showing up authentically, or are you playing a role to please others? Have a conversation with a friend or partner where you express your true feelings, desires, and boundaries without worrying about their reaction.
- **Example:** If you've been holding back in a friendship, openly share something that's been on your mind, even if it feels vulnerable. Notice how it impacts the connection.

7. EXERCISE: RELEASE THE FEAR OF JUDGMENT

- **Goal:** Let go of the fear of judgment and focus on inner validation.
- **How:** For one week, whenever you feel the urge to censor yourself due to fear of judgment, pause and acknowledge the feeling. Then, choose to act in a way that aligns with your values, even if it feels uncomfortable. Reflect at the end of the day on how it felt to release the fear of judgment and how it impacted your actions.
- **Example:** If you have a tendency to avoid speaking your mind in a group for fear of being judged, push yourself to share one thought or idea that you might typically keep to yourself. Reflect on how the experience shifts your sense of self-worth.

8. JOURNALING PROMPT: THE IMPACT OF BEING AUTHENTIC

- **Goal:** Reflect on how authenticity positively affects your life.

- **Prompt:** Write about a time when you were able to be your true self and how that impacted the situation, your relationships, or your emotional well-being. How did being authentic make you feel? What was the outcome?
- **Example:** Think of a time when you finally expressed your true feelings in a difficult conversation. How did it feel to speak your truth, and what changed in your relationship as a result?

9. EXERCISE: CREATE AN AUTHENTICITY AFFIRMATION

- **Goal:** Strengthen your commitment to embracing authenticity.
- **How:** Write a daily affirmation that reinforces your commitment to living authentically. Make it personal and empowering. Each morning, read your affirmation aloud and repeat it when you feel challenged or uncertain about showing up as your true self.
- **Example:** An affirmation could be: "I am worthy of being seen for who I truly am, and I release the need for approval. I trust myself to make decisions that align with my authentic self."

10. EXAMPLE: LETTING GO OF THE NEED FOR APPROVAL

- **Goal:** Shift your focus from seeking approval to honoring your truth.
- **How:** Reflect on a recent situation where you sought approval or tried to please others. Recognize the underlying desire for validation, and practice letting go of that need. Instead, focus on how you can show up authentically without the need for external validation.
- **Example:** If you caught yourself tailoring your social media posts to impress others, consider how you can share something more aligned with your true thoughts or passions—without worrying about likes or comments. Notice how it feels to let go of that need for approval.

By consistently practicing these exercises and reflecting through journaling, you will begin to strengthen your authenticity muscle and release the pressures of external expectations. The more you embrace your true self, the more peace, freedom, and confidence you will experience, aligned with the core principles of the Let Them Principle.

CHAPTER 5

Cultivating Resilience and Inner Peace

TECHNIQUES TO STOP WASTING ENERGY ON OTHERS

Many of us expend an incredible amount of mental and emotional energy trying to control or manage the behavior of others. We have a propensity to try to influence other people's behaviors, attitudes, or responses to fit our own needs and preferences, whether they be friends, family, coworkers, or even complete strangers. This is frequently done unintentionally, driven by an instinctive need to keep control over our surroundings and the people that inhabit them. However, we lose sight of what really matters—our own development and mental well-being—when we concentrate on controlling other people.

The secret to ending this loop is to turn our attention from other people to ourselves. Inspired by Mel Robbins' teachings, the Let Them Principle urges us to let go of our control over other people's actions and concentrate on our own personal development. By grasping this idea, we may begin focusing our energies on developing our own tranquility, self-assurance, and personal development rather than squandering them trying to manage the uncontrollable.

First, be aware of where you're spending your time and thoughts to stop wasting energy on others. The first step to change is awareness. Start by identifying the times you find yourself obsessing over the choices or behaviors of others. Do you ever find yourself reliving discussions in an attempt to understand what other people were thinking? Are you caught up in attempting to sway someone's decisions? The procedure starts with identifying these patterns. When you find yourself attempting to control someone else's behavior, you can instantly redirect your attention to yourself by asking, "What can I do for myself right now? What aspects of myself do I need to improve or learn?

Practicing detachment is the next tactic. Giving others the freedom to be who they are without tying their behavior to your own sense of serenity or self-worth is what it means to be detached, not to shut off your feelings or become uncaring about other people. Although it can be difficult in relationships where you have invested a lot of emotional energy, detaching will allow you to use that energy for yourself. You can start to accept that others will behave in ways that are influenced by their personal experiences once you let go of the impulse to exert control.

Developing mindfulness is a beneficial way to shift your attention from other people to yourself. Being mindful enables you to live in the present without passing judgment or responding. Mindfulness enables you to concentrate on the present moment rather than letting your thoughts wander to ideas of how you could improve someone else. Breathing techniques, meditation, or even simple pursuits like going for a stroll or sipping tea can all help you cultivate mindfulness. You recover energy that would have been used to control or worry about someone else each time you practice being totally present.

Adopting the idea of limits is another way to quit wasting energy on other people. Establishing sound boundaries is a crucial ability that lets you know where you stop and other people start. It gives you the ability to stand firmly in your own space without assuming the emotional burdens of others by helping you identify what you are and are not ready to tolerate. Your boundaries may be too flimsy if you are often attempting to control the feelings or actions of others. You may quit wasting your energy on things that aren't your responsibility by explicitly stating and clarifying your boundaries.

The practice of self-compassion is equally vital. You are frequently ignoring your own needs and well-being when you are preoccupied with controlling or improving other people. Learning to treat yourself with kindness can lead to personal development and self-improvement. Treating yourself with the same consideration, tolerance, and forgiveness that you would extend to a friend is a key component of self-compassion. Instead of wasting time criticizing yourself when you fail or make mistakes, try to be compassionate. This boosts your self esteem and provides you with the emotional room you need to develop and change without having to exert control over anything else.

Concentrating on your personal objectives and passions is another effective strategy. We lose sight of our goals when we become preoccupied with the decisions made by others. Turn your attention to your own development, aspirations, and ambitions. What thrills you? What do you have a strong interest in? You automatically stop investing time and effort in other people's lives when you concentrate on your own goals and aspirations. Compared to the draining endeavor of managing others, this will produce a sense of completion and self-empowerment that is far more satisfying.

Another important strategy is to learn to let go of expectations. We frequently squander energy by clinging to preconceived notions about what other people ought to say, do, or act under particular circumstances. These demands are a kind of control that binds you to other people's behavior. You can avoid needless annoyance and disappointment by letting go of these expectations and accepting individuals for who they are. You give yourself the freedom to accept others for who they are, without attempting to alter them, when you stop expecting them to satisfy your needs or desires.

Sometimes concentrating on appreciation is the best strategy to quit wasting energy on other people. You instantly cut down on the emotional energy you spend on things that are beyond your control when you alter your emphasis from attempting to influence or change other people to enjoying what you have. You may concentrate on the good things in your life instead of the things you wish were different when you are grateful. Simply writing down three things for which you are thankful each day might serve as this practice. Making thankfulness a habit helps you develop a positive outlook that turns your energy inward and promotes development.

Lastly, accept the strength of release. Letting go is a continuous process of deciding to trust life's process and letting go of the demand for control. You will feel more at ease and liberated the more you practice letting go. It just indicates that you no longer let other people's actions control your emotions, not that you no longer care about them. Letting go enables you to focus your energies on your own personal development, inner peace, and self-love—areas where you can truly make an impact.

By using these strategies, you can stop squandering valuable energy on attempting to influence other people. You will spend less time and energy controlling other people the more you engage in your own personal development. Greater independence, peace, and confidence are the natural results of living in accordance with the Let Them Principle.

Here are some useful activities, examples, and writing prompts to help you put the "Let Them Principle" into practice and quit wasting energy on other people:

EXERCISE 1: ENERGY DRAIN AWARENESS

Consider for a moment when and how you use your emotional energy to attempt to influence or transform other people. Keep a record of every time you find yourself attempting to control, alter, or correct someone else's conduct for a day. Jot down the circumstances, the things you were attempting to control, and your feelings. Be aware of these moments because awareness is the first step to refocusing.

EXERCISE 2: THE REDIRECT PRACTICE

Stop for a moment and deliberately refocus your energies if you notice that you are concentrating on the actions of another person. "What can I concentrate on that supports my development and tranquility at this moment?" Next, decide on an activity that advances your own personal growth, such as picking up a new skill, working on a project, or even just taking a break for self-care. Refocusing your attention on yourself will naturally help halt the energy drain, so make it a habit.

EXERCISE 3: THE BOUNDARY SETTING

In a relationship, when you spend a lot of effort trying to alter someone else, set a straightforward, unambiguous limit. If a friend keeps interrupting you, for instance, politely tell them, "I appreciate our conversations, but I need to finish my thoughts without being interrupted." Without attempting to influence the other person's response, practice establishing this boundary with confidence and love. This will allow you to regain your energy while still honoring the autonomy of other individuals.

EXERCISE 4: RETHINKING JUDGMENT

Ask yourself, "Is this judgment coming from a place of control?" the next time you find yourself passing judgment on someone else's choices or behavior. If so, attempt to reframe your thinking by concentrating on how you may enhance your own behavior or attitude rather than attempting to alter theirs. For the benefit of both you and the other person, try letting go of judgment and adopting a more sympathetic viewpoint.

EXERCISE 5: SHIFT IN GRATITUDE

Write down three things about your life and personal development for which you are thankful at the end of each day. Small victories, personal development, or instances where you made decisions that improved your own well-being might all fall under this category. By concentrating on thankfulness, you can return your attention from outside distractions and exhausting thoughts about other people to enjoying your own trip.

PROMPTS FOR JOURNALING:

1. Consider a moment when you were preoccupied with attempting to dictate the behavior of another person. How did you feel emotionally at the time? What impact did it have on your energy and sense of calm?

2. Write about a relationship that leaves you feeling exhausted most of the time. How can you maintain your energy without feeling guilty by establishing boundaries?

3. Consider a recent instance in which you made a behavioral judgment about someone. How could you have focused on something more personal development-friendly?

4. When you concentrate solely on yourself, where in your life do you feel most at peace? In what other aspects of your life can you incorporate these techniques?

5. What are three actions you can take right now to shift your focus from other people to your own development?

You will start to see where they are wasting energy on other people and how they might recover that energy for their own development, self-assurance, and inner serenity by doing these activities and thinking about the prompts.

SHIFTING FOCUS TO WHAT TRULY MATTERS

We frequently lose sight of what really matters in life because of the never-ending pressure to succeed, live up to expectations, and balance obligations. Many people find it simple to lose themselves in the cacophony of social pressures and outside demands. The ability to turn our attention from the things that divert us to the aspects of life that actually bring us happiness, development, and inner fulfillment is the key to attaining serenity and long-lasting fulfillment. The "Let Them Principle" provides a clear means to accomplish this goal on this trip by teaching us to let go of the urge for control and have faith that what is important will come to the fore. Focusing on what truly merits our attention is made possible by letting go of outer expectations, judgments, and distractions.

Finding the places where our attention has been diverted is one of the first steps in changing our focus. It's critical to recognize that we frequently let other people's wants and opinions dictate our priorities. We pressure ourselves to meet demands at the expense of our goals, aspirations, and health. Our focus can be readily diverted from the things that are genuinely important by the pressure to follow trends, live up to others' expectations, or reply to incessant social media updates. We must examine how we now use our energy and sincerely question ourselves, "Is this serving my personal growth?" in order to alter this dynamic. Does this reflect my true values?

Consider what makes you feel fulfilled as a starting point for determining what is important. What gives you a sense of purpose, joy, and peace is more important than what other people think is successful or what society considers successful. It's simple to fall into the trap of conducting our lives in accordance with outside standards, but changing our focus necessitates asking ourselves, "What activities make me feel alive?" Which connections help me grow? What accomplishments, independent of approval from others, make me proud of myself?

This investigation frequently yields unexpected discoveries. The things we've been spending the most time on are probably not the ones we think are most important. For instance, a person may discover that while spending time with family makes them feel deeply fulfilled, their days are taken up by exhausting social or professional commitments. When we start to pay attention to our inner compass, we are motivated by what we know would make our lives more fulfilling rather than what other people think we should prioritize.

Effectively setting priorities is the next obstacle after determining what really matters. This entails establishing a distinct set of ideals that serve as your compass. Your values act as an internal framework that guides your decision-making and boundary-setting. Saying no to things that don't fit with your beliefs is made easier when you know what is most important to you. Saying "no" is a crucial skill when it comes to changing focus. Filtering out the noise that doesn't add to your pleasure or personal development is more important than completely dismissing people or obligations.

One effective way to start setting priorities is to apply the "90/10 Rule." This rule is straightforward but very powerful. This theory suggests spending 90% of your time and effort on what matters most to you and 10% on what doesn't or doesn't fit your values. Prioritize spending time with loved ones before overcommitting to work, errands, or social gatherings, for instance, if you value family time. Making the distinction between what is important and what is just a diversion is made easier by the 90/10 Rule.

Another tactic is to let go of the urge for control or perfection by adopting the "Let Them Principle" approach. We frequently waste needless energy striving for perfect outcomes in every area of our lives or finding it difficult to live up to others' expectations. Dissatisfaction and burnout may result from this. Refocusing entails letting go of the need to live up to every expectation and realizing that perfection is a myth. We are able to invest in the aspects of life that truly please us after we let go of these expectations. In addition to lowering stress, letting go of this need for control allows us to experience greater levels of contentment.

Our approach to work-life balance serves as an illustration of this idea. Many people become fixated on work-related duties, trying to get everything just right. We may lose out on important personal experiences because of this urge, including spending time with our loved ones or engaging in pastimes that feed our passions. We can change our emphasis by letting go of the desire to manage every part of our work lives and allowing ourselves to be present in the moments that are actually important outside of work by putting the Let Them Principle into practice. This could entail learning to assign responsibilities, establishing clear boundaries between work and personal time, and having faith that everything will work out if we don't have continual control.

Being mindful can greatly help with focus shifting in addition to letting go of control. Being completely present in the here and now, free from distraction and judgment, is the essence of mindfulness. We cease thinking about pursuing the next objective, assignment, or approval when we engage in mindfulness practices. Instead, we learn to appreciate what we have right in front of us, whether it's a quiet moment of introspection, a talk with a buddy, or an enjoyable pastime. Being mindful helps us connect with what really matters, in addition to bringing us back to the present. We can develop a stronger bond with the things that make us content and fulfilled if we give our whole attention to the experiences we are having right now.

Finally, cultivating thankfulness on a regular basis might help you change your perspective. We start to develop a mindset that puts an emphasis on the things that are already valuable to us when we regularly show gratitude for the people, events, and accomplishments in our lives. By turning our emphasis from what we lack to what we have, gratitude enables us to concentrate on abundance rather than scarcity. Whether it's a simple morning stroll, the freedom to follow a passion, or a thankful buddy, thankfulness helps us stay focused on the important things in life.

Focusing on the important things is a continuous process rather than a one-time event. Intentionality, introspection, and a readiness to break harmful habits are necessary. We can choose to focus on the aspects of life that bring us calm, growth, and confidence by adopting the "Let Them Principle," which frees us from the effect of outside demands and judgments. In the end, we make room for a life full of joy, honesty, and meaning by purposefully rerouting our energy. In keeping with the "Let Them Principle" from Mastering the Power of Let Them: A No Nonsense Guide to Peace, Freedom, and Confidence, these useful activities, examples, and journaling prompts are intended to assist you in refocusing your attention on the things that are most important in their lives. Inspired by the Teachings of Mel Robbins:

PRACTICAL EXERCISES

1. Audit of Energy: Every night, take a moment to consider how you spent the day. Jot down the things that consumed your time and energy. Next, consider whether they were in line with your personal priorities. Did you concentrate on things that will help you be content and healthy in the long run? Were there individuals or things that diverted you from your main priorities? You'll be able to spot trends and make space for the important things with the help of this activity.

2. Exercise in Prioritization: List your five most important values, which could be peace, creativity, career, health, family, and personal development. Now consider how much time you spend on these principles every day or every week. Does a balance exist? In what areas of your life could you refocus your attention to prioritize those that are consistent with your values? For the next week, make a conscious effort to focus more on these topics.

3. Apply the "90/10 Rule" to change your attention. Decide that 90% of your energy will be focused on activities that are consistent with your fundamental values and 10% will be allocated to less important chores in any particular scenario or week. Start by making minor adjustments to your relationships, career, or leisure time. Experience the change in attention and its effect on your inner peace.

4. Using the "Let Them" strategy: Get better at letting go of things you can't control. For example, take a step back and tell yourself, "Let them," if you find yourself worrying over someone else's actions. To feel at peace, you don't have to exert control over other people. Acknowledge the energy you can save by concentrating on your reaction rather than attempting to influence the other person. For instance:

1. Moving Away from Social Expectations: Take the example of someone who, although finding social occasions exhausting, feels compelled to go to them in order to blend in with their peer group. This person may start turning down invitations and instead devote themselves to things that rejuvenate them, such as a solitary stroll or an in-depth discussion with a friend, by refocusing their attention on what really matters—possibly personal time or fostering close relationships. They are able to prioritize their actual demands over those of society.

2. Work-Life Balance: Picture someone who is always feeling overburdened at work and who aspires to be perfect and get their boss's favor. By using the "Let Them Principle" and understanding that their value is independent of approval from others, individuals can establish boundaries at work by assigning chores to others and refusing requests when they are needed. They can restore equilibrium and tranquility by refocusing on the things that are most important, such as family, personal endeavors, or self-care.

3. Healthy Relationships: Trying to "fix" other people or being in toxic relationships can sap a person's emotions. By applying the "Let Them Principle," individuals let go of the impulse to dictate what other people do. They recognize that their energy is best spent with individuals who share mutual respect and understanding, so they prioritize connections that support them and establish clear boundaries with those that don't.

JOURNALING PROMPTS:

1. Identifying What Matters:

- What are the top 5 things that, if nothing else, would make you feel fulfilled in life? (These could be relationships, personal goals, hobbies, etc.)
- How often do you prioritize these things in your daily life?
- What distractions or outside pressures keep you from focusing on these? How can you minimize or let go of these distractions?

2. Releasing Control:

- Reflect on a situation where you are trying to control an outcome. How does this impact your peace of mind?
- Write about the people or situations where you feel the urge to take control. What might happen if you chose to let go and allowed things to unfold naturally?

3. The Power of Boundaries:

- Think about a recent time when you said "yes" to something out of obligation, even though it didn't align with your true priorities. How did this make you feel?
- How could you have responded differently, in a way that honored your values and your time? Write a script of how you could handle a similar situation in the future.

4. Reassessing Your Commitments:

- Are there commitments in your life that no longer align with your core values? Write about them and why you're still holding onto them.
- What can you do to gently release these commitments? What might you be able to replace them with that would bring more peace and fulfillment?

5. Setting Intentions for the Week:

- As you prepare for the upcoming week, write down three intentions you want to focus on. These should be aligned with your values and what truly matters to you.
- How will you ensure that you stick to these intentions throughout the week, and what will you do if distractions arise?

"The Let Them Principle" teaches us the art of relinquishing control and acknowledging that we cannot make everything fit into our plans, but it is not about ignoring obligations. We can begin to recover our time and energy through hands-on activities and the application of straightforward yet effective techniques like mindfulness, prioritization, and boundary setting. We may start to create a life that is more in line with who we really are by consistently checking in with our values, letting go of distractions, and mastering the art of saying "no" when it's appropriate. As you learn to change your emphasis to what really matters, this approach will help you find more confidence, independence, and peace.

CREATING A CALM AND CENTERED MINDSET

It sometimes seems impossible to find moments of calm in our hectic lives. We continually balance obligations, interpersonal relationships, and personal objectives while dealing with outside distractions and demands. However, when we step back, we see that by using basic stress-reduction and grounding strategies, we may develop inner calm and a centered mentality. Finding balance and developing a tranquil mind need us to learn to let go of the things we cannot control and concentrate on what is really important.

It takes deliberate work to cultivate a calm and composed mindset; it doesn't happen instantly. In Mastering the Power of Let Them, we accept the notion that attempting to manage circumstances beyond our control is a major source of stress in our life. We may create space for greater tranquility, independence, and self-assurance when we learn to let go.

Stress is one of the biggest barriers to mental clarity. Stress doesn't only occur during major events; it frequently results from a buildup of minor stresses that we ignore. This ongoing low-level stress can seriously impair our mental health by leaving us feeling disorganized, preoccupied, and emotionally spent. We can take charge of our mental health and lessen the effects of daily stress by identifying these stressors and building a toolkit of strategies to combat them. Recognizing the value of quiet is the first step toward developing a composed and focused mentality. There is a lot of noise in our everyday life, whether it comes from the surroundings or from our incessant worries and thoughts. It's challenging to access our inner calm and clarity when we're not still. Although mindfulness and meditation are effective techniques for promoting mental calm, they may appear overpowering to people who have never used them. For this reason, beginning modestly—just a few minutes every day—can be a terrific way to get started.

For cultivating quiet, the "5-minute mindful check-in" is a straightforward activity. Set a five-minute timer and find a quiet place to sit at any time during the day. Shut your eyes, inhale deeply, and start observing your thoughts objectively. Simply observe them without attempting to alter or manipulate them. Bring your attention back to your breathing softly if your thoughts stray. When done regularly, this simple exercise can help teach your mind to slow down and focus on the here and now.

Deep breathing is another effective method for cultivating a relaxed attitude. Our breath is a constant companion and an instant instrument for relaxation. Just paying attention to our breathing can instantly lower tension and help us return to the present. The "4-7-8 technique" is a useful deep breathing technique. Breathe in deeply through your nose for four counts, hold it for seven counts, and then gently exhale through your mouth for eight counts to complete this exercise. After a few minutes of repeating this pattern, you'll notice that your body and mind are starting to calm down.

Gratitude exercises, in addition to deep breathing, are an effective method of changing your perspective to one of calmness. We automatically divert our attention from tension and negativity when we concentrate on the things for which we are thankful. Even under trying circumstances, gratitude enables us to rediscover serenity and reframe our experiences. Spend a few minutes at the end of each day writing down three things for which you are thankful. They should be sincere, regardless of their size. This straightforward exercise strengthens a focused and peaceful attitude and teaches your brain to focus on the good.

Another crucial element of stress management is physical activity. Exercise improves mental health in addition to physical health. Moving our bodies helps us decompress and encourages the release of endorphins, which are naturally occurring mood enhancers. Find a movement that you enjoy, whether it's yoga, dancing to your favorite music, or taking a stroll. Including regular exercise in your routine helps you retain inner calm and mental clarity in addition to improving your physical health.

The Let Them Principle's core concept of "letting go" can be applied to the process of developing a composed and focused attitude. We frequently cling to things that no longer benefit us, such as poisonous relationships, unresolved disputes, or the urge to be in charge of every area of our lives. In order to relieve ourselves of needless worry, we must let go of these things. This means we stop attempting to force results and let go of the drive for perfection, not that we neglect our obligations or lose interest in significant relationships. We come to accept life as it comes and have faith that everything will work itself out.

Journaling is one way to assist in letting go. You can process and let go of your feelings by putting your ideas, anxieties, and fears in writing. It's similar to leaving a bulky bag behind after unloading it. Don't hold back when writing in your journal; just let your ideas come to you. After you've written everything down, consider what you're clinging to and whether it still serves your needs. What can you give up to create room for clarity and tranquility?

The practice of "non-attachment" is another beneficial activity. This entails developing the ability to disengage from the results of events and individuals. It's about embracing life's uncertainties and letting go of the need to control everything, not about giving up or accepting defeat. Ask yourself, "What would it feel like if I released my attachment to this outcome?" if you're feeling overpowered by a scenario. You could discover that your tension subsides and that you can address the matter with greater composure and clarity. Setting boundaries is the last strategy for developing a composed and focused mindset. Setting limits is crucial for preserving our emotional and mental well-being and averting fatigue. We often take on too much because we're afraid of disappointing others or can't say "no." But one approach to respecting ourselves and our needs is to learn how to set appropriate limits. Learn to say "no" when it's necessary, and don't feel negative about putting your health first. You may conserve your energy and concentrate on the things that really matter by establishing boundaries.

It takes constant effort and the ability to let go of things that don't benefit you to develop a peaceful and balanced mentality. You can lessen stress and develop inner peace by including these practices into your everyday routine: writing, letting go, non-attachment, gratitude, deep breathing, physical activity, mindfulness, and boundary-setting. We create serenity within ourselves, not outside of ourselves. A more concentrated, tranquil, and satisfying life becomes possible when we concentrate on the things we can manage and let go of the rest.

The Let Them Principle teaches us that embracing life as it is, without attempting to control every aspect, is the path to true freedom and confidence. You may stop wasting energy on things that don't matter and develop a mindset that promotes your well-being by putting these strategies into practice and mastering the art of letting go. You will feel more joy, freedom, and peace as you let go of unneeded tension and concentrate on what really matters.

CHAPTER 6

Practical Applications of The Let Them Principle

AT WORK: NAVIGATING TOXICITY AND MANAGING EXPECTATIONS

At work, we often face stress, expectations, and pressures that come from both the organization and our colleagues. Managing these stressors can be particularly challenging in toxic circumstances or when we are confronted with unreasonable expectations. Applying the *Let Them Principle*—which is all about giving up control over things that aren't yours to handle—is essential to being composed, grounded, and self-assured in these circumstances. You concentrate on preserving your own tranquility and personal development rather than attempting to alter other people or surroundings.

There may be toxic environments, difficult coworkers, or problematic personalities at work that can sap your vitality and leave you feeling overburdened. You may feel trapped and unable to succeed due to a micromanaging supervisor, passive-aggressive coworkers, or incessant requests from higher management. One of the most frequent errors we make is attempting to alter or correct others around us in the hopes that everything would improve if we could just "convince" them to behave differently. But this is a pointless effort. The truth is that we have no control over the behavior or attitudes of others. We are in charge of our responses and how we protect our own health.

The Let Them Principle becomes crucial in this situation. You can relieve yourself of needless emotional and mental strain by coming to terms with the fact that you cannot alter other people. You gain the ability to control your own expectations, maintain composure, and defend your boundaries. This mental change is effective because it frees you from internalizing the negative aspects of your job, giving you more energy to concentrate on the things you can control, such as your own behavior, reactions, and personal development.

Putting this theory into practice at work starts with setting limits. Setting limits is essential for mental health and avoiding overcommitment. The sense that you must always say "yes" to requests, even when doing so places undue pressure on you, is a major source of stress at work. After receiving unclear or unreasonable demands, you may feel overwhelmed and unsure how to meet them. Instead of accepting every task or attempting to please everyone, think about whether it fits with your role, abilities, and values.

In case your manager asks you to do something outside your job description or workload, don't be afraid to say you need to prioritize first. It's crucial to express politely but assertively that you need to know exactly how much work you have before committing to anything new. This is a self-care practice that safeguards your time and mental health. By admitting your time and energy are limited, you're not rejecting the assignment.

This strategy is also applicable when interacting with coworkers who could put demands on your time or behave toxically. Remind yourself that you can only manage your response, not your emotions or your attempts to "fix" their conduct. It's not necessary for you to take in their negativity. It can be immensely freeing to let go of the need to alter someone's mindset or conduct. For instance, you don't need to become involved in the drama if a coworker is impolite or contemptuous. Instead of becoming defensive or attempting to change their opinion, just decide not to join in the negative. React professionally, calmly, and assertively, and then stop there. You give yourself the ability to be unaffected when you don't let other people's actions control how you feel.

Concentrating on your personal growth is another strategy for handling stress in poisonous situations. This entails spending money on your development and welfare as opposed to squandering time attempting to alter the workplace. No matter where you go, you will run into poisonous behavior, obstacles, and negativity since the workplace is a reflection of the wider society. You turn your attention within rather than on the actions of others. Pay attention to how you can develop despite the circumstances around you. Applying the Let Them

Principle effectively means putting less emphasis on the things you cannot control and more emphasis on developing your abilities and self. Developing a greater sense of self-worth, improving emotional intelligence, or improving communication skills could all be part of this.

Growth, not perfection, should always be the main goal. Nobody is flawless, and most workplaces aren't perfect. However, by learning to concentrate on your own growth, you free up your mind to handle challenging circumstances with greater clarity and less emotional exhaustion. Develop the practice of routinely reflecting on your development, whether it be by journaling, practicing mindfulness, or asking for input from others. Regardless of outside obstacles, this change in perspective gives you a sense of empowerment and confidence.

Knowing when to leave situations that no longer benefit you is another crucial component of putting the Let Them Principle into practice at work. Leaving is sometimes the best course of action when dealing with poisonous situations or unrealistic expectations. Being honest with yourself about whether the work environment is worth the toll it's having on your health and well-being is more important than instantly leaving your job. It might be time to reconsider if this position or company is a good fit for you if you find yourself feeling exhausted, anxious, or dissatisfied all the time. When a change is necessary, don't be scared to follow your gut.

It's important to remember that not all workplaces are toxic or coworkers are difficult. In various situations, you may be coping with sporadic annoyances or miscommunications. When this occurs, it's critical to analyze the situation using the Let Them Principle. Are you upset with a coworker because you have certain expectations about their behavior? Or is it predicated on what they did? We frequently cause tension by clinging to irrational notions about how other people ought to treat us. We release ourselves from the ongoing disappointment and annoyance that accompany these expectations when we let them go. This implies letting go of the desire to dictate how other people behave, not reducing standards, or putting up with unacceptable behavior.

The best course of action when you are subjected to unreasonable expectations at work is to deal with them immediately. Sometimes coworkers or managers have unreasonable expectations of you, presuming you can handle more than is reasonable. Instead of complying with every request, stand back and consider whether the demands are realistic. Discuss reasonable expectations openly with your manager. It's preferable to voice your worries rather than allowing the stress to mount if you're feeling overburdened by the workload. You may avoid burnout and set more reasonable expectations for both yourself and other people by being honest about your capabilities.

We stop internalizing other people's behavior when we stop attempting to influence their actions. We no longer waste energy trying to achieve impossible standards or modify them. We begin concentrating on how we can be the best versions of ourselves and cease worrying about what other people think. The key to implementing the Let Them Principle in the workplace is this change in viewpoint. You regain control of your tranquility and self-assurance by concentrating on your own reaction, boundaries, and development. You learn to prioritize your own well-being over allowing outside pressures to control your mood.

In conclusion, it might be challenging to deal with toxic workplaces and unreasonable demands, but by using the Let Them Principle's tenets, harmony can be preserved. You can establish a work atmosphere that promotes your mental health by focusing on personal development, letting go of the impulse to control others, and establishing appropriate boundaries. You turn your focus inward and embrace what you can control, such as your reaction, your behavior, and your attitude, rather than attempting to mend the things that are broken around you. If you apply this, you'll find you can succeed despite any obstacles.

Here are some useful activities, examples, and journaling prompts to help you use the Let Them Principle to manage expectations and navigate toxicity at work. These exercises promote a mental shift toward confidence, freedom, and calm.

1. Setting Boundaries with Toxic Colleagues

- **Exercise:** Identify a toxic behavior at work (e.g., gossiping, micromanaging, passive-aggressiveness). Reflect on how this behavior affects your peace and productivity. Write down one specific boundary you can set to protect yourself from this behavior (e.g., limiting communication with a specific colleague, addressing inappropriate behavior directly but respectfully).
- **Example:** If a colleague constantly interrupts your work with trivial matters, set a boundary by letting them know you're available to talk only during specific times, and stick to it.
- **Journaling Prompt:** "What is one toxic behavior I tolerate at work that affects my well-being? What boundary can I set to protect my energy?"

2. Managing Unrealistic Expectations

- **Exercise:** Write down a recent situation where you were overwhelmed by unrealistic expectations. Reflect on what you could have done differently if you had applied the Let Them Principle. How can you clarify or negotiate expectations to maintain your peace?

- **Example:** If your manager asks for a project on short notice, instead of saying yes right away, pause and assess your workload. Communicate your current priorities and negotiate a realistic deadline.
- **Journaling Prompt:** "When have I taken on too much at work? How can I manage expectations more effectively next time?"

3. Releasing Control Over Others

- **Exercise:** Think of a colleague whose behavior or performance frustrates you. Write down how you might be trying to control or change their actions. Then, write down how you can release this need for control and focus only on what you can change—your own responses and actions.
- **Example:** If a colleague is late to meetings, instead of trying to change their habits, accept that you can't control their behavior. Focus on how you prepare for meetings, making sure you're ready and unaffected by their tardiness.
- **Journaling Prompt:** "What colleague's behavior do I try to control? How can I focus on controlling my own responses instead?"

4. Self-Awareness and Reflection

- **Exercise:** At the end of each day, reflect on how you reacted to toxic situations or unrealistic expectations. Write down what worked (keeping your peace, setting boundaries, etc.) and what didn't. Use this reflection to adjust your approach for the next day.
- **Example:** If you found yourself stressed after a challenging meeting with your boss, take a moment to breathe, release the tension, and assess how you could have handled it differently (e.g., speaking up for your needs or taking a break afterward).
- **Journaling Prompt:** "How did I handle stress or toxic behavior at work today? What could I have done differently to stay centered?"

5. Developing Emotional Detachment

- **Exercise:** Choose one stressful situation at work (e.g., a difficult conversation, a challenging project). Practice emotional detachment by observing the situation without emotionally reacting. Focus on your breath and remind yourself that their actions or opinions are not your responsibility.
- **Example:** If a colleague criticizes your work, instead of feeling personally attacked, pause, breathe, and assess the feedback objectively. Detach emotionally from the criticism and use it for improvement, without letting it define you.
- **Journaling Prompt:** "What was a recent stressful situation I faced at work? How can I detach from emotions and observe the situation with clarity?"

6. Cultivating a Growth Mindset

- **Exercise:** Identify one area where you feel stuck or overwhelmed at work. Write down a positive affirmation that reflects your belief in your ability to grow and handle challenges. Practice repeating this affirmation throughout the day, especially in moments of stress.
- **Example:** If you're struggling with a new project or responsibility, instead of feeling defeated, remind yourself: "I am capable of learning and handling challenges. I am growing with each experience."
- **Journaling Prompt:** "What is one area at work where I feel stuck? How can I shift my mindset to embrace growth instead of stress?"

7. Mindful Breathing and Centering Techniques

- **Exercise:** During moments of high stress at work, practice mindful breathing for two minutes. Breathe in deeply for four counts, hold for four counts, exhale for four counts, and repeat. This helps calm the mind and restore clarity.
- **Example:** If you're about to enter a meeting with high stakes, take a few moments before it begins to center yourself with mindful breathing. This reduces stress and allows you to stay calm and focused.
- **Journaling Prompt:** "When was the last time I felt overwhelmed at work? How can I use mindful breathing to regain control and stay calm?"

By applying these exercises and prompts, you'll learn to navigate workplace challenges with a clear sense of peace and empowerment. The Let Them Principle encourages you to stop absorbing toxic behavior and unrealistic expectations, and instead, focus on what you can control: your mindset, your boundaries, and your growth. This approach not only reduces stress but also fosters an environment where you can thrive personally and professionally.

IN LOVE: STRENGTHENING ROMANTIC RELATIONSHIPS

Understanding your own needs and having the flexibility to accept your spouse for who they are both essential to developing a happy, healthy romantic relationship. The intricacies of a relationship, such as demands, expectations, and communication difficulties, can easily cause one to lose sight of the essential notion that each of us has unique identities. As a manual for tranquility, independence, and self-assurance, the Let Them Principle can change the dynamics of your relationship and make love not just simpler but also more pleasurable and profound.

The ability to genuinely let go of the things we attempt to control is at the core of any successful relationship. Control frequently takes the form of the desire to alter our partner's behavior or even control our emotions toward them, especially in love relationships. We all have preconceived notions about how our spouse ought to act—whether those preconceptions relate to their communication, affection, or contribution to the partnership. However, these expectations—which are frequently based on our own worries or insecurities—can restrict the relationship's ability to develop.

Learn to use the Let Them Principle to realize how important it is to accept your partner as they are. The capacity to let go of these domineering inclinations makes room in relationships for real love and connection. Couples can start embracing their individuality rather than trying to change one another or impose unattainable norms. To develop intimacy and trust, you must accept your partner's flaws, peculiarities, and differences. Both of you will have greater freedom in your relationship the more you realize how important it is to let your partner be who they are.

This does not include putting up with disrespect or letting go of important limits. It entails recognizing that attempting to change your partner or exert control over their behavior only results in annoyance and bitterness. You may make room for both spouses to thrive, separately and jointly, by deciding to let go of that need for control. By letting go of the little things that don't contribute to the greater scheme of love, this mentality change enables you to concentrate on the things that truly count—connection, support, respect, and shared ideals. Understanding that growth happens via mutual respect and shared experiences rather than constant control or change is the cornerstone of any healthy romantic relationship. Relationships are about two flawed individuals who value one another's uniqueness and strive for mutual enjoyment and development, not about producing the ideal person or dynamic. The Let Them Principle gives each partner room to continue being unique while still developing as a couple.

Deeper, more satisfying conversation becomes possible when you stop trying to dictate your partner's every action. Communication becomes dominated by attempts to control or influence one another, which leads to the breakdown of many relationships. Partners stop being vulnerable, open, and honest and instead focus on how to communicate in ways that shield them from criticism or conflict. Your talks will be more genuine and caring once you let go of the impulse to be in charge. You foster an atmosphere in which everyone may express their own emotions without worrying about criticism or rejection.

Stronger emotional ties and the capacity to resolve challenging problems together result from this.

Letting go of your personal insecurities is another essential component of using the Let Them Principle in your love relationship. Relationships frequently suffer when one or both partners have feelings of inadequacy or rejection anxiety. These fears could be the result of early life events, previous relationships, or social pressures. However, feeling in control of one's emotions or continuously looking to a partner for approval can lead to excessive stress in a relationship. You can let go of the need for continual assurance or outside validation when you apply the Let Them Principle to your own emotions. By believing that your value is independent of other people's behavior, you let your spouse be themselves without worrying about how their actions may affect your sense of self.

Avoiding challenging conversations is not the same as letting go of the impulse to manipulate or correct your partner. Instead, it entails addressing difficult subjects with an attitude that prioritizes learning and development over correcting. You can communicate your feelings about your partner's behavior from a place of empathy and understanding rather than from one of judgment or blame. Both parties can feel heard and appreciated when you accept responsibility for your own feelings and communicate honestly, which lessens the possibility of defensiveness or confrontation. Disagreements are not seen as dangers to the relationship but rather as chances to get to know one another better and strengthen the bond between the two of you.

The capacity to accept imperfection is one of the most potent facets of letting go in romantic relationships. Relationships and individuals are not flawless. There will always be disagreements, miscommunications, and difficulties in any partnership. However, you make space for grace when you let go of perfectionism, whether it's the belief that your partner will always satisfy your wants precisely as you desire or that everything should always be in harmony. This gives both partners the opportunity to make errors, grow from them, and help one another through life's ups and downs.

Strong relationships are characterized by how well two individuals collaborate to overcome obstacles rather than how well they meet expectations. By accepting one another's weaknesses, forgiving one another's errors, and demonstrating unwavering love even under trying circumstances, they develop trust. Accepting that genuine, enduring love is messy and flawed—and that's what makes it wonderful—is the capacity to let go of perfectionism without giving up on the connection.

The more you relax from outside pressures, the better your relationship will be. Unrealistic expectations are frequently placed on love relationships by society, ranging from how partners should behave to how they should look to how fast they should advance. When you let go of these outside influences, you can concentrate on what really matters: the special connection you have with your spouse. The media, family, and friends frequently have their own notions about what love should look like. Without having to worry about what other people think, you can define your relationship however you see fit.

Accepting your own personal development within the framework of a partnership also entails letting go of the pressure to live up to outside expectations. To be a successful spouse, you don't have to give up on your own aspirations, and you shouldn't expect your partner to do the same. However, helping each other achieve their goals will help the relationship and each person thrive. You both give each other the freedom to be genuine and fulfilled when you let go of cultural norms that limit your potential.

The biggest transformation in your intimate connection, according to the Let Them Principle, occurs when you stop seeking your partner's approval or changing all the time. You create an environment where you and your partner can thrive without criticism or expectations by focusing on your own behaviors, emotions, and open, loving communication. Alternatively, you can just be who you are, encouraging each other's development and establishing a relationship based on love, respect, and common principles.

A stronger, more durable relationship results from this change toward relinquishing control, controlling your fears, accepting imperfection, and letting go of outside influences. As a result, you'll find that love may be the most rewarding and liberating feeling of all when it is not bound by expectations.

In line with the values of tranquility, liberty, and self-assurance derived from Mel Robbins' teachings, the following useful activities, illustrations, and journaling prompts will assist you in implementing the Let Them Principle in your romantic relationships:

EXERCISE 1: IDENTIFY YOUR EXPECTATIONS VS. REALITY

Objective: To recognize and release unrealistic expectations you might be placing on your partner.

Instructions:

- Take a moment to write down a list of expectations you have for your partner. These could be related to how they show affection, their behavior, or even their future goals.
- Next, reflect on how these expectations align with reality. Are they achievable or fair? How might they create unnecessary pressure in the relationship?
- Finally, write down how you might release or adjust these expectations to focus on fostering love and connection without demanding perfection.

Journaling Prompt:

"Think about a time when I tried to change my partner or had an unrealistic expectation of them. How did this affect our relationship? How can I shift my approach to accept them for who they are?"

EXERCISE 2: LETTING GO OF CONTROL IN CONFLICT

Objective: To practice managing conflicts by releasing the need to control your partner's reactions.

Instructions:

- The next time you find yourself in a disagreement, take a deep breath and focus on controlling your own response instead of trying to control how your partner reacts.
- Write down the emotions you experience in the moment. How do you feel when you realize that you cannot control your partner's behavior? How can you communicate your needs while still respecting their autonomy?
- After the conflict, reflect on the outcome. Did releasing control lead to a healthier discussion? What could you do differently next time?

Journaling Prompt:

"When was the last time I tried to control the outcome of a disagreement with my partner? How can I let go of the need to control and allow space for them to have their own feelings and responses?"

EXERCISE 3: EMBRACING IMPERFECTION IN YOUR PARTNER

Objective: To shift from perfectionism to acceptance in your partner's flaws.

Instructions:

- Write down one thing about your partner that bothers you. Acknowledge that this trait, whether big or small, does not define their worth.

- Reflect on the positive qualities that you love and appreciate about your partner.
- Make a conscious decision to focus on the positive rather than trying to change the negative aspects. What can you do to embrace this imperfection without judgment?

Journaling Prompt:

"How can I embrace my partner's imperfections without trying to change them? In what ways has their uniqueness brought value to our relationship?"

EXERCISE 4: ENCOURAGING AUTONOMY IN YOUR RELATIONSHIP

Objective: To create a supportive, balanced relationship where both partners feel free to be themselves.

Instructions:

- Think about areas in your relationship where you may have unintentionally overstepped or controlled your partner's decisions or actions.
- Create a list of ways you can encourage your partner's autonomy and support their personal growth.
- Try to implement one of these actions this week—whether it's giving them space for their hobbies, supporting their career goals, or trusting their decisions without interference.

Journaling Prompt:

"In what ways can I support my partner's independence while still being emotionally available for them? What is one area where I can give them more freedom this week?"

EXERCISE 5: SHIFTING FOCUS FROM NEEDS TO CONNECTION

Objective: To move away from focusing on what your partner should do for you, and focus more on how you can foster a deeper connection.

Instructions:

- Write down any needs or wants you've been placing on your partner, such as expectations around affection, attention, or communication.
- Now, turn your focus inward and write about what you can bring to the relationship. How can you show up more authentically and attentively, without focusing on getting something in return?

- Practice making small changes in how you approach interactions. Shift from "What can they give me?" to "How can I contribute to this relationship?"

Journaling Prompt:

"What does it look like when I focus more on connection and less on my needs in the relationship? How can I prioritize shared experiences over fulfilling my expectations?"

EXERCISE 6: CELEBRATING YOUR PARTNER'S STRENGTHS

Objective: To strengthen the relationship by appreciating your partner's qualities and how they contribute to the dynamic.

Instructions:

- Spend a day focusing on your partner's strengths. Take note of the qualities you admire—whether it's their sense of humor, their creativity, or their kindness.
- Share these observations with them in a thoughtful way. Let them know how these qualities positively impact your life and the relationship.
- Focus on nurturing the aspects of the relationship that you cherish, rather than fixating on flaws or things you wish were different.

Journaling Prompt:

"What are the strengths I admire most in my partner? How can I show appreciation for these qualities more often? How can these strengths positively shape our relationship moving forward?"

EXERCISE 7: PRACTICING GRATITUDE IN LOVE

Objective: To deepen the connection by practicing gratitude and expressing appreciation in the relationship.

Instructions:

- Take time each day to reflect on one thing you are grateful for about your partner, whether it's something they did or simply their presence.
- Share your gratitude with them in a meaningful way—whether through a note, a text, or a heartfelt conversation.
- Reflect on how expressing gratitude changes the energy in your relationship. Do you feel more connected? Do you notice positive changes in your interactions?

Journaling Prompt:

"What is one thing I am grateful for in my partner today? How does expressing gratitude deepen my connection with them? How can I show more appreciation for them in the future?"

EXERCISE 8: SETTING BOUNDARIES WITH LOVE

Objective: To understand the importance of setting healthy boundaries while maintaining respect and love.

Instructions:

- Reflect on any boundaries that are either being crossed or are unclear in your relationship. This could include time, space, or emotional needs.
- Write down the boundaries you need to establish for your well-being. These could include personal time, emotional space, or communication needs.
- Practice expressing these boundaries to your partner in a clear and loving manner, focusing on your needs without blaming or criticizing them.

Journaling Prompt:

"What boundaries do I need to set to feel more balanced in my relationship? How can I express them in a way that fosters mutual respect and understanding?"

EXERCISE 9: FOSTERING EMOTIONAL SAFETY

Objective: To create a space of emotional safety in your relationship, where both partners feel comfortable sharing their true selves.

Instructions:

- Think about how safe you feel expressing your emotions and vulnerabilities in your relationship. Are there areas where you feel hesitant or afraid to open up?
- Write down ways you can create emotional safety, such as listening without judgment, validating each other's feelings, and being open to difficult conversations.
- Practice being more vulnerable with your partner, sharing your thoughts, fears, and desires, while creating space for them to do the same.

Journaling Prompt:

"How can I create a safer emotional space for both myself and my partner? In what ways can I encourage vulnerability and honesty without fear of judgment or rejection?"

EXERCISE 10: RELEASING EXPECTATIONS OF CHANGE

Objective: To embrace your partner exactly as they are, freeing both of you from the pressure of needing to change for love.

Instructions:

- Reflect on any areas where you've hoped for change in your partner, whether it's behavior, habits, or perspectives.
- Recognize the difference between supporting growth and needing to change your partner. What would it feel like to let go of the pressure for them to change?
- Consciously practice acceptance by embracing your partner's current self, and acknowledge that true love comes from accepting each other as you are.

Journaling Prompt:

"What is one thing I've been trying to change about my partner? How can I release that expectation and embrace them as they are? How would accepting them fully transform our relationship?"

These exercises, examples, and journaling prompts will help guide you in applying the Let Them Principle to your romantic relationship. By focusing on acceptance, appreciation, and personal growth, you create a more loving and authentic connection with your partner, fostering peace and confidence in both yourself and your relationship.

WITH FAMILY AND FRIENDS: LETTING GO OF UNREALISTIC DEMANDS

It's all too simple to become caught up in the burden of unreasonable expectations in our relationships with friends and family. These demands can feel overpowering, regardless of whether they stem from the need for unwavering attention, implicit expectations, or the need to be someone we're not. These pressures frequently stem from the implicit belief that it is our responsibility to attend to everyone else's demands without considering our own, rather than from malice. Regaining our own independence, cultivating positive relationships, and maintaining inner calm all depend on our ability to let go of these unreasonable expectations. By using the Let Them Principle, you may develop relationships based on respect and understanding by learning how to set boundaries that let you show up for people in a way that respects their needs as well as yours.

Understanding that other people's expectations of you, whether they be friends, family, or coworkers, are frequently based on their own wants and perceptions is a key component of the Let Them Principle. You are not responsible for carrying or managing these. Even if they think they need something from you, never let them make you unhappy. You take a critical step toward regaining your independence and peace the instant you acknowledge that you cannot please everyone and that their expectations are not your burdens. Naturally, the difficulty is in doing this in a way that fosters mutual respect and understanding rather than friction in your relationships.

Begin by acknowledging that people's expectations of you are shaped by their personal experiences and perspectives. These expectations can occasionally result from the roles that people have grown to expect you to fulfill. Perhaps you are viewed as the "responsible one," the "peacekeeper," or the "assistant." If we let these roles define who we are, they can become restrictive. It's critical to consider if you have genuinely accepted these responsibilities or if they were only thrust upon you for the convenience of others. We frequently take on these roles in order to win acceptance, steer clear of conflict, or because we've been socialized to believe that's what other people need from us. But when you understand that you don't have to play these parts in order to be liked or valued, that's when true serenity starts.

Developing awareness is a terrific method to begin releasing the hold on these unreasonable demands. Be aware of when other people's expectations are causing you to feel overburdened or worn out. When you really want to say no, do you feel compelled to say yes? Do you consistently prioritize the needs of others before your own? These emotions are signs that the demands made of you are unsustainable and unhealthy. More awareness of these situations will improve your ability to stop, assess the situation, and decide whether to take responsibility. According to the Let Them Principle, you should just accept the circumstances and declare, "This is not for me," without feeling bad or guilty about your decision.

Learning to say no is another useful tactic for letting go of unreasonable requests. Saying no is about asserting your boundaries and prioritizing your needs, not rejecting others. In the beginning, saying no can be hard, especially if you've been saying yes to everyone. But it's essential for your mental and emotional health. Start by practicing saying no in little ways. It could be telling a friend that you can't assist with a project they want you to work on or turning down an invitation to an event that you know will sap your energy. You'll begin to experience the sense of liberation that comes from being in charge of your time and energy with every no.

It's especially difficult to break free from irrational expectations in family connections. Family interactions are frequently complicated, and there may be a long-standing conviction that family members should support one another no matter what. However, family doesn't mean you have to put others before yourself. Family members may want you to be there for every event or to offer unwavering emotional support, but it's acceptable to stand back if you're feeling overburdened, burned out, or overextended. Providing love and care when you are truly available is what gives your presence in their life meaning, not your demands.

Having frank, caring discussions is one method to begin establishing boundaries in family interactions. For instance, be honest about your circumstances if a family member persistently requests your assistance in a way that is exhausting. "I would love to be there for you, but I need to take care of myself right now," or "I can't take on that responsibility at the moment, but I can help in other ways," are some examples of suitable statements. Being honest about your limitations makes you a healthy and honest family member, not a negative one. This helps provide room for others to step up when necessary since it establishes a clear standard that you can only offer what you are able to give.

Since we frequently anticipate a certain degree of intimacy and assistance, the demands can occasionally feel even more challenging when they relate to friends. Unspoken pressure to be consistently available, in touch, or willing to drop everything is common. Although having strong, encouraging pals is great, it's crucial to realize that these connections don't have to come at the expense of your own tranquility or mental space. Genuine friendships are based on respect and understanding between the two people, not on scorekeeping or completing a never-ending to-do list.

Talking openly about your requirements is one of the best ways to ease the strain of unreasonable demands in friendships. Inform your friend politely and plainly if they are always asking for help but you are unable to provide them with the time and attention they require. While letting them know you're available, be reasonable about how frequently you can interact. Saying, "I care about you, but I'm going through a lot right now," could be a straightforward method to deal with this. I'm here for you when I can, but I can't be as available as I usually would be. By being honest and forthright, this method not only respects your personal space but also sustains the friendship. The more you do this, the simpler it will be to control expectations and maintain the relationship's integrity.

In addition to others' expectations, we sometimes set unreasonable ones for ourselves. We can believe that we must always be the "ideal" friend, relative, or spouse, always going above and beyond what we can provide. But we eventually burn out when we live up to these expectations we put on ourselves. The Let Them Principle encourages us to practice self-compassion and let go of these self-imposed expectations. Your value is not based on how much you offer or how well you live up to other people's expectations, and you don't have to be everything to everyone. When you let go of being "perfect," you allow yourself to be human with all your flaws and limitations.

In conclusion, finding balance means letting go of unreasonable expectations in your friendships and family. It's about being truthful with both yourself and other people, seeing that you don't have to save people, and realizing that genuine relationships are based on respect rather than duty. By assisting you in concentrating on what really matters—your freedom, your boundaries, and your well-being—the Let Them Principle provides a straightforward yet effective framework for fostering harmony in your relationships. Put these ideas into practice to create healthier, more satisfying relationships that help you and your loved ones thrive.

PRACTICAL EXERCISES

To help readers apply the Let Them Principle in managing unrealistic demands from family and friends, here are some practical exercises, examples, and journaling prompts designed to foster healthy boundaries, reduce stress, and promote peace.

EXERCISE 1: IDENTIFY UNSPOKEN EXPECTATIONS

- Write down a list of people in your life—family members, close friends, and anyone else you frequently interact with.
- For each person, jot down the unspoken or unrealistic expectations you feel they place on you. For example, do they expect you to always be available

for them? Do they have certain assumptions about how much you can give emotionally or physically?

- Reflect on each expectation and assess whether it's something you've willingly accepted or if it's something you've felt pressured into. Recognize that these expectations aren't necessarily your responsibility.

Example:

You may realize that your sibling expects you to drop everything when they call because they feel overwhelmed, but you might be managing your own responsibilities. Acknowledge this pattern and gently recognize that while you care for your sibling, you are not obligated to always be their emotional caretaker.

EXERCISE 2: PRACTICE SAYING "NO"

- Start by practicing small no's. You don't have to jump into large, confrontational moments right away. Instead, begin by saying no to small requests.
- For example, if a friend invites you to a social event when you feel you need rest, simply say, "I appreciate the invite, but I need to take some time for myself this weekend."
- This exercise helps you recognize that saying no does not diminish the value of the relationship, but instead shows respect for your own needs.

Example:

Perhaps your friend asks you to attend a last-minute gathering. Instead of feeling obligated, say something like, "Thanks for thinking of me, but I can't make it this time. Let's catch up soon." This keeps the boundary intact without guilt.

EXERCISE 3: SETTING BOUNDARIES WITH COMPASSION

- Reflect on your relationships where you often feel overwhelmed by others' demands. Identify one specific person where you could set a healthy boundary.
- Write down a clear, compassionate message that communicates your need for space, time, or a limitation.
- Example message: "I love spending time with you, but I can't always be available every weekend. I need some time to recharge, but I'd love to find another time that works for both of us."

Example:

If a family member expects you to always be the go-to for babysitting, you could say, "I'm happy to help when I can, but I can't do it every weekend. I need time to focus on other priorities, but we can plan something in advance for the next time."

EXERCISE 4: CREATE A PERSONAL BOUNDARY INVENTORY

- In a journal, write down situations where you've felt overwhelmed or taken advantage of by family or friends. Reflect on how those situations could have been handled differently if you had stronger boundaries.
- For each situation, note how you might have set a healthier boundary using the Let Them Principle. For example, if a friend constantly borrows money without returning it, your boundary could be that you'll no longer lend money unless you're okay with the potential outcome.

Example:

If you've been agreeing to help with family projects even when you feel drained, you could set a boundary that you'll only commit to things that align with your current energy and time. This empowers you to manage your capacity and to prioritize your own well-being.

EXERCISE 5: REFLECTION JOURNALING

- Set aside 10 minutes each day to journal about your experiences with family and friends. Focus on how you feel when unrealistic demands are placed on you.
- Ask yourself questions like:
  - How did I feel when I said yes to this request?
  - Did I feel resentful, stressed, or overwhelmed?
  - How could I have responded differently to respect my needs and boundaries?
- By reflecting on these moments, you start recognizing patterns and become more aware of situations where you might need to set limits.

Example:

You might realize that you often agree to host family gatherings, even though it's stressful for you. Journaling about this might reveal that you're seeking approval or avoiding conflict, and you can start to rewrite this pattern by setting a boundary next time and suggesting alternative ways to spend time together.

EXERCISE 6: ENVISION YOUR IDEAL RELATIONSHIPS

- Take some time to visualize what your ideal relationships with family and friends would look like. How would you communicate? How would you manage their expectations? How would they respect your boundaries?
- Visualizing these ideal interactions can help you see that healthy relationships are based on mutual respect, not on constant sacrifices.
- Write a detailed description of these ideal relationships and how you would interact when someone places an unrealistic demand on you.

Example:

Imagine you're at a family dinner, and a relative asks you to take on a project that's not in your capacity. In your ideal relationship, you calmly express your needs, stating, "I can't do that right now, but I'd be happy to help in another way." Visualizing this scenario helps reinforce the idea that it's possible to say no without damaging the relationship.

EXERCISE 7: DAILY AFFIRMATIONS

Create a set of affirmations that reinforce your right to set boundaries and prioritize your well-being. These affirmations help you stay grounded in your decision to let go of unrealistic demands.

Examples of affirmations:

- "I honor my own needs and set healthy boundaries with love."
- "I am worthy of respect, and my time is valuable."
- "It's okay to say no and still have strong relationships."
- "I release guilt when I prioritize my well-being."

Example:

Say these affirmations each morning to remind yourself of your right to live without constant pressure. Repeating these will help you internalize the message that boundaries are a healthy, necessary part of maintaining peaceful relationships.

EXERCISE 8: ROLE-PLAYING SCENARIOS

- Role-playing with a friend or a trusted person can be a helpful way to practice how to handle uncomfortable situations where you might feel pressured to say yes.

- Pick a scenario where you often struggle to set boundaries, such as someone asking you for favors you can't accommodate. Practice saying no or explaining your need for personal space.
- After role-playing, debrief with your partner to see how it felt and adjust the approach based on their feedback.

Example:

You could role-play with a friend the situation where a family member asks for an unreasonable favor. Your partner could be the family member, and you practice calmly saying, "I can't commit to that right now, but I'd love to help in other ways."

These exercises, when practiced consistently, will help you break free from the cycle of unrealistic demands. By reflecting, setting boundaries, and communicating honestly with those closest to you, you will create relationships that respect both your needs and theirs. The Let Them Principle teaches us that we are not obligated to fulfill every expectation placed on us, and by letting go of those unrealistic demands, we make room for healthier, more fulfilling connections.

CHAPTER 7

Designing a Life You Love

PRIORITIZING YOUR GOALS
OVER EXTERNAL NOISE

n today's world, distractions are more pervasive than ever before. It might be challenging to stay focused on personal objectives when faced with the incessant barrage of notifications, peer pressure to fit in, or the deluge of outside viewpoints. But the secret to living the life you want is learning to tune out the distractions and focus on what really counts. At this point, the Let Them Principle becomes a crucial instrument for promoting freedom, tranquility, and self-assurance. Relieving pressure to meet external expectations lets you focus on your true goals.

Prioritizing your objectives over outside distractions requires first understanding the distinction between the voices that attempt to sway you and your internal compass. The opinions of friends and coworkers, family expectations, and social pressures are frequently the sources of our distractions. These factors are empowered to cloud our judgment, causing us to second-guess our choices, give up on our goals, or squander time on activities that are inconsistent with our moral principles.

Taking a minute to reflect on oneself is the first step toward conquering this obstacle. What are my goals, you ask? What long-term and short-term goals do I really want to accomplish? Being self-aware allows you to make decisions based on your values and vision rather than others' expectations. According to the Let Them Principle, you should accept outside influences but resist letting them dictate your choices. It is up to you to determine what is most important.

Set your goals with clarity and purpose after determining them. The SMART goal-setting methodology is among the best ways to achieve this. Specific, Measurable, Achievable, Relevant, and Time-bound are the acronyms for SMART. This framework gives you clear direction without the debilitating sense of ambiguity that frequently accompanies outside distractions by breaking down big, intimidating goals into smaller, more attainable steps. Start with the SMART framework's "Specific" section. Avoid nebulous objectives like "I want to be successful" or "I want to be healthier" when you're making goals. Instead, make specific, doable objectives like "I will commit to a weekly exercise routine in order to lose 10 pounds" or "I will finish a certification in digital marketing by the end of this year." It's simpler to monitor your progress and maintain focus on the activities that will help you reach these specified goals.

Making sure your goals are "measurable" is the next step. This implies that you require a method for determining whether or not you are improving. One module per week could be used to gauge your progress toward the digital marketing certification. Maintaining a diet and activity journal or monitoring weekly weigh-ins could be quantifiable goals for weight loss. These quantifiable benchmarks foster accountability and facilitate motivation maintenance in the face of outside distractions.

"Achievable" goals are ones that you can actually accomplish. Setting unattainable goals can lead to failure and despair, particularly when you're surrounded by outside noise that could cause you to doubt your skills. For instance, it might be excessively ambitious to set a goal of losing thirty pounds in a month if you're just beginning to exercise. Rather, begin with modest, more achievable objectives, like reducing two to three pounds a month, and then progressively raise them as you make progress.

Additionally, your objectives must be "relevant," which means they must complement your overarching life vision. Realizing that not all external expectations line up with your true objectives is a key component of the Let Them Principle. You might be tempted to follow the newest trends or someone else's definition of success, but doing so frequently results in frustration and fatigue. You must choose what is most important to you, for example, if your family is pushing you toward a more conventional career path in business or law even though your passion is to work in a creative profession. Being relevant means choosing meaningful and rewarding goals over what others think you should do.

Lastly, your objectives should be "time-bound," which entails establishing a reasonable deadline for completion. Without due dates, it's simple to become distracted by other things or to put things off indefinitely. You give yourself a sense of urgency and give your goals a concrete form by making a timeline. Establish deadlines for each task if you want to finish a certification by year's end. This helps you stay on course and keeps outside distractions from sabotaging your advancement.

Even in the face of distractions, using the SMART framework to set goals helps you stay focused on what is really important. Setting goals by itself, however, won't help you stay on course as pressure from outside sources increases. If you want to stay focused, you must also form solid habits that support your dedication to your objectives.

Setting daily priorities is one effective habit. Spend a few minutes each day thinking about your objectives and determining the most crucial things you need to get done that day. Divide your lofty goals into smaller, daily tasks to achieve them with this method. Setting priorities also keeps conflicting demands on your time from overwhelming you. For instance, you might prioritize your professional development duties in the morning when you have more energy and concentrate on your workout later in the day if you're pursuing both a job and a personal fitness objective.

Creating a "distraction-free" area is another useful tactic. To guarantee that you have unhindered time to concentrate on your objectives, this may include establishing limits with family members or coworkers. Distractions from social media, emails, and phone notifications are common in the current digital era. You may set up specified times for monitoring social media and email or disable notifications during particular hours of the day to save time. You can improve your productivity and maintain focus on your objectives by getting rid of or cutting down on distractions.

It's important to learn how to tune out outside noise in addition to controlling distractions, particularly when it comes from others who might have different opinions on your life's purpose. You may probably come across criticism or unsolicited advice while you work toward your own objectives. Selective listening is the secret to staying focused. Even if constructive criticism is helpful, it's crucial to disregard unfavorable remarks or suggestions that don't support your goals. The Let Them Principle gives you the confidence to follow your gut and let other people's viewpoints go by without allowing them to stop you from moving forward.

Developing a "mental filter" for outside information is one method to do this. When someone makes remarks or offers advice that doesn't further your objectives, just accept their viewpoint without taking offense. "That's their viewpoint, but I'm focused on my path," you may be thinking. This mental filter will eventually become an effective tool for keeping your attention on task and blocking out outside distractions.

Learning how to handle obstacles and disappointments is a crucial part of setting priorities. It's simple to get disheartened and sidetracked by disappointment when things don't work out as planned. But any path to achievement will inevitably include failures. Use these challenges as chances to develop and learn rather than letting them make you doubt your objectives or give up completely. When you encounter a setback, stand back and evaluate the circumstances. What does it teach you? How can you modify your strategy to proceed? You may maintain focus on your long-term objectives by considering setbacks as transient difficulties rather than permanent obstacles.

Finally, it's critical to acknowledge and appreciate your accomplishments, no matter how minor. Recognizing even the slightest accomplishments encourages you to keep going and strengthens your resolve to achieve your objectives. Take a time to acknowledge your efforts when you reach a milestone or cross a task off your list. Even when there are other distractions vying for your attention, celebrating your accomplishments keeps you inspired and concentrated. In conclusion, if you want to create the life you want, you must put your ambitions ahead of outside distractions. You may stand out from the crowd and succeed for a long time by defining specific, doable goals, forming daily routines, ignoring outside distractions, and remaining committed to your own course. The main ideas of the Let Them Principle are self-confidence and letting go of outside pressures. Mastering this way of thinking makes room for calm, independence, and self-assurance, which enables you to remain dedicated to your objectives in spite of outside distractions.

The following useful activities, illustrations, and writing prompts will assist you in implementing the Let Them Principle in your everyday life and giving your objectives precedence over outside distractions:

EXERCISE 1: IDENTIFYING EXTERNAL NOISE

- **Goal:** Identify sources of external noise that distract you from your personal goals.
- **Instructions:** Take a few minutes to list the voices or pressures around you—family, friends, social media, colleagues, societal expectations—that affect your ability to focus on what matters most. Write down how these voices influence your decisions, actions, and priorities.

- **Reflection:** Now, use the Let Them Principle to release the weight of these influences. Acknowledge their existence but choose not to let them control you. How can you create space for your own voice to lead your journey?

EXERCISE 2: DEFINING YOUR TRUE PRIORITIES

- **Goal:** Set clear, actionable goals based on your true desires, not external demands.
- **Instructions:** Write down three to five personal goals you are passionate about. These should be goals that feel aligned with your values and vision, not those shaped by outside pressure. Ensure that these goals are specific, measurable, achievable, relevant, and time-bound (SMART).
- **Reflection:** Look at the goals you've written. Are there any that you've set because of others' expectations? How can you adjust them to be more in line with your true priorities?

EXERCISE 3: CREATING A "DISTRACTION-FREE" ZONE

- **Goal:** Build habits that protect your time from distractions.
- **Instructions:** Choose one hour of your day to dedicate solely to working on your goals without interruption. During this time, turn off notifications, limit social media use, and set clear boundaries with family and friends about your time.
- **Reflection:** After completing your "distraction-free" hour, write about your experience. How did it feel to have uninterrupted focus on your goals? What external influences were the hardest to ignore, and how did you manage them?

EXERCISE 4: SAYING "NO" TO NON-ESSENTIAL DEMANDS

- **Goal:** Learn how to say no without guilt in order to protect your time and energy.
- **Instructions:** Reflect on recent situations where you said "yes" to requests or invitations out of obligation rather than desire. Identify a situation where you could have said "no" to protect your goals. Practice saying "no" to a non-essential request this week, and instead, dedicate that time to your personal priorities.
- **Reflection:** After the experience, journal about how it felt to say no. Did it feel empowering or uncomfortable? How can you continue to set healthy boundaries to prioritize your goals?

EXERCISE 5: VISUALIZING YOUR IDEAL DAY

- **Goal:** Clarify how you want to spend your time based on your priorities.
- **Instructions:** Imagine your ideal day where you are fully focused on your goals and free from distractions. Write a detailed description of this day,

including the activities, people, and actions involved. Be specific about how you spend your time, your mindset, and the steps you take toward your personal goals.

- ▪ **Reflection:** Compare your ideal day with your current reality. What is currently blocking you from living this ideal day? How can you adjust your routine to make this vision more attainable?

Example 1: The Power of Daily Prioritization

- **Situation:** Jane is a career-driven woman with a passion for starting her own business. However, she often gets sidetracked by her friends' social events and family obligations. Every time she works on her business plan, she feels overwhelmed by the constant demands from others.

- **Application of Let Them Principle**: Jane starts by recognizing that she can't please everyone, and she decides to prioritize her business goals. She sets aside 30 minutes each morning before work to focus on her business plan. Over time, she also learns to say no to unnecessary commitments, giving her the freedom to focus on her goals.

Example 2: Managing External Expectations from Family

- **Situation:** Mark has always wanted to pursue a career in graphic design, but his family insists he should take a more "stable" job in finance. He often feels torn between honoring his family's expectations and following his own passion.

- **Application of Let Them Principle:** Mark acknowledges the love and concern his family has for him but realizes their expectations are based on their own fears and beliefs, not his personal goals. By practicing the Let Them Principle, Mark decides to continue pursuing his design career and sets boundaries with his family about his choices. He communicates his goals clearly, knowing that he must prioritize his passion to live a fulfilled life.

JOURNALING PROMPTS:

1. What external voices have the most influence over my choices, and why do I give them power?

2. When I think about my goals, do they reflect my true desires, or are they shaped by what others expect of me?

3. How can I start saying "no" to external demands that do not align with my priorities?

4. What would my ideal day look like if I spent all my time focused on my personal goals?

5. What are three actionable steps I can take this week to prioritize my goals over external distractions?

By integrating these exercises, examples, and journaling prompts into your daily life, you can effectively apply the Let Them Principle to prioritize your goals, eliminate distractions, and create a life filled with focus, freedom, and the confidence to follow your own path.

DAILY PRACTICES TO STAY IN CONTROL OF YOUR ENERGY

Establishing daily routines that support your ideals, improve your mental clarity, and cut down on pointless distractions is crucial to keeping your energy under control and preserving your sense of inner freedom and tranquility. No matter what outside demands you face, these routines serve as a foundation that keeps you focused and centered.

Developing awareness in your daily life is the first step. More than just meditation, mindfulness involves being aware of every action you make throughout the day. Being present in the moment, whether it be when eating, strolling, or conversing, means that you are preventing distractions from taking over your thoughts. Just spending five minutes each morning checking in with yourself, recognizing your physical and mental well-being, and noting any ideas that may be going through your head can be a basic daily mindfulness practice. You establish the tone for the day and develop an awareness-based habit that keeps you in charge of your energy by doing this on a regular basis. Making a conscious start to your day is another important habit. The morning routine establishes the tone for the rest of the day. Take a moment to consider what is really important, rather than getting out of bed and rushing into life's hectic schedule. Put your top three objectives or goals for the day in writing. Choosing to remain composed at a challenging meeting or resolving not to overcommit yourself could be examples of this. You take charge of your day and lessen the likelihood that you will be distracted by other factors when you have clear aims.

Another effective strategy for keeping your energy under control is exercise. Emotional equilibrium and mental clarity are directly impacted by physical activity. Stretching, yoga, or a quick walk can help you clear your head and feel better without requiring a strenuous workout. Frequent exercise aids in the body's natural release of tension, which can lead to stress and anxiety. Exercise also promotes the body's natural feel-good chemicals, endorphins, to be produced. You may significantly improve your mood throughout the day by moving for a few minutes each day.

Making it a habit to prioritize your health by getting enough sleep and rest is equally vital. In our fast-paced society, sleep is frequently underestimated, despite the fact that it is essential for preserving stable emotions and a clear, sharp intellect. It's crucial to establish a bedtime routine that encourages rest and improved sleep. This can entail reading a book, listening to relaxing music, or shutting off screens an hour before bed. Maintaining regular sleep hygiene guarantees that your body and mind are adequately rejuvenated, enabling you to awaken with the vitality required to face the day with clarity and concentration.

Another essential element of energy protection is setting boundaries. One of your most effective tools is the ability to say no. People have expectations of you in your personal and professional life, and without limits, you may feel overburdened. Saying no is not a sign of rejection; rather, it is a way to save time and effort. To keep your peace, you must acknowledge that you cannot satisfy everyone's needs and that doing so will exhaust you. Spend some time every day thinking about any situations where you need to improve your boundaries and practicing saying no when it's appropriate.

Reducing outside distractions is another behavior that has a direct impact on your energy levels. Distractions abound in the digital age. Text messages, emails, and social media can divert your focus from what is really important. Instead of reacting to notifications right away, you might establish specific periods throughout the day to check these platforms. This prevents you from being pushed in numerous directions all the time and helps you stay focused on the here and now. You can also cut back on the negative news and poisonous situations that sap your energy. You have more energy control when you limit exposure to non-supportive items.

Practicing gratitude on a regular basis might change your perspective and save your energy. Your mind starts to concentrate on the positive aspects of your life rather than the negative ones when you actively seek out things for which you are thankful. Practice thankfulness at the beginning and finish of each day. In the morning, list three blessings. This small deed can make your entire day more positive. At night, go back on your day and write down the happy or peaceful moments, no matter how minor they may have been. Being grateful keeps your energy levels high and attracts more positive things into your life.

One way to maintain focus during the day is to practice mindful breathing. Breathe deeply a few times when you feel anxious or overwhelmed. If you can, close your eyes. Take a deep breath for four counts, hold it for four counts, and then gently release it for four counts. By resetting your neurological system, this simple breathing technique can help you de-stress and relax. By scheduling a full meditation period in the morning or evening, you can also integrate deep breathing into your everyday routine. You can manage your energy by mastering your breathing.

Developing a self-compassion practice is another habit. It's simple to become preoccupied with other people's needs and forget about your own. But it's crucial to ask oneself, "What do I need right now?" on a daily basis. This might be as simple as taking a moment to relax or engaging in something enjoyable. Self-care is not selfish; rather, it is essential. By filling your own cup first, self-compassion allows you to fully present yourself to others without compromising your own tranquility.

Finally, stop trying to be flawless. Because it demands you to always prove yourself and live up to irrational expectations, perfectionism is an energy drain. Aim for advancement rather than perfection. You relieve yourself of the pressure you put on yourself when you concentrate on giving it your all without expecting perfection. You are free to pursue your objectives without needless worry thanks to this mentality change.

Consistency is crucial in all of these behaviors. Even when you don't feel like it, it's crucial to include these daily rituals in your routine since habits are formed via repetition. You actively shape your energy when you begin your day with intention, schedule physical activity, set boundaries, and cultivate thankfulness. You will feel more at ease and liberated the more you do this and the more control you have over your inner state.

You may build a strong foundation for serenity, independence, and confidence in your life by accepting responsibility for your energy and prioritizing your daily routine. Although you can't control everything in your life, you can control your reaction. With the knowledge that your energy is yours to preserve and develop, these exercises equip you with the skills to react with poise and assurance.

Here are some useful activities, examples, and writing prompts to help you apply the Let Them Principle to your everyday life in order to keep your energy under control and your inner peace:

1. Morning Mindset Practice:

- **Exercise:** Upon waking, take 5 minutes to sit in silence. Close your eyes and check in with yourself: How do you feel physically and emotionally? Acknowledge any tensions or thoughts and then choose to let them pass without judgment. Set a simple intention for the day, like "Today, I choose calm and clarity."
- **Journaling Prompt:** "What is one thing I can focus on today that aligns with my personal goals, and how can I guard my energy against distractions?"

2. Physical Activity Breaks:

- **Exercise:** Schedule short, 5-minute physical activity breaks throughout your day. Whether it's a quick walk, stretching, or yoga, moving your body helps clear mental fog and resets your energy. You don't need a structured workout routine—just a quick release of physical tension to stay grounded.
- **Journaling Prompt:** "When I take a break to move, how does my body feel afterward? What energy shifts have I noticed?"

3. Boundaries Check-In:

- **Exercise:** Throughout the day, pay attention to any moments where you feel drained or overwhelmed by others' expectations. Pause and ask yourself, "Is this mine to handle?" If not, consciously decide to let it go or communicate your limits in a kind but firm way.
- **Journaling Prompt:** "What demands from others am I currently absorbing that are draining my energy? How can I gently set boundaries to reclaim my peace?"

4. Digital Detox:

- **Exercise:** Pick a time each day, such as an hour after waking up or before going to bed, to disconnect from all digital devices. Use this time for self-reflection, reading, or engaging in a calming activity that centers you.
- **Journaling Prompt:** "How do I feel when I disconnect from the digital world? What emotions or thoughts arise when I'm not constantly checking my phone or email?"

5. Gratitude Practice:

- **Exercise:** Start or end your day by listing three things you are grateful for. These don't need to be grand—simple things like a hot cup of coffee or a moment of laughter can shift your focus from stress to appreciation.
- **Journaling Prompt:** "What are three things I am grateful for today? How does practicing gratitude impact my energy levels?"

6. Breathing for Calm:
- **Exercise:** Whenever you feel overwhelmed, pause and practice a 4-4-4 deep breathing technique: Inhale for 4 seconds, hold for 4, and exhale for 4 seconds. This helps release tension and reset your mental state.
- **Journaling Prompt:** "After taking several deep breaths, how do I feel? How does this small practice shift my focus and energy?"

7. Intentional Scheduling:

- **Exercise:** Each morning, review your schedule and ask yourself, "What will take the most energy today, and how can I approach it with calm?"

Prioritize tasks that align with your values and delegate or say no to those that drain your energy.

- **Journaling Prompt:** "What tasks or meetings are coming up today that will require a lot of energy? How can I approach them with calmness and clarity?"

8. Self-Compassion Break:

- **Exercise:** If you notice negative self-talk or feelings of guilt for not meeting expectations, stop for a moment. Remind yourself that it's okay to not be perfect. Practice a moment of kindness by saying something supportive to yourself, like "I am doing my best, and that's enough."
- **Journaling Prompt:** "When was the last time I showed kindness to myself? How can I show myself more compassion today?"

9. Evening Reflection:

- **Exercise:** At the end of the day, reflect on moments when you felt peaceful and in control of your energy. Celebrate those moments of clarity, and note any situations where your energy was drained. Consider what adjustments you can make for tomorrow.
- **Journaling Prompt:** "What moments today made me feel at peace? How can I carry that energy into tomorrow?"

10. Release Unnecessary Expectations:

- **Exercise:** Each evening, take a moment to think about anything you might be holding onto—whether it's an unrealistic expectation from others or a personal goal that feels out of reach. Write down one thing you're willing to release, acknowledging that it's not necessary for your peace.
- **Journaling Prompt:** "What expectation am I holding onto that's draining my energy? How can I release it without guilt?"

By consistently practicing these exercises, you'll learn to protect your energy and create a sense of peace and balance in your life. This allows you to stay focused on what truly matters and filter out the distractions and pressures that don't serve your well-being. Through the daily application of these principles, you'll gain more control over your emotions, reduce stress, and develop a stronger sense of inner calm and freedom.

LIVING WITH INTENTION AND JOY

deciding to live a joyful and purposeful life begins with deliberately focusing your energies on the things that are most important to you. All too frequently, responsibilities, outside demands, and diversions engulf people in the maelstrom of everyday life. However, we regain control when we embrace the power of intention. We decide how to live our lives on our own terms, independent of what other people think or demand. Inspired by Mel Robbins, the Let Them Principle is a straightforward yet deep method for bringing our thoughts, deeds, and emotions into harmony to build peaceful, independent, and self-assured lives.

Knowing that we have the ability to influence our experiences is at the heart of living purposefully. Reacting to the situations around us and allowing outside noise to influence our feelings and choices is a common mistake. But a change is necessary to live consciously. Determining our response, focusing on what we can control, and letting go of the rest is key.

Beginning to live consciously requires determining your priorities. Step back and consider your principles, aspirations, and objectives. What gives you a sense of fulfillment? What does success mean to you? Though they might not appear right away, these solutions will start to emerge with some reflection. Clearly define your priorities. You may start making choices that support your goals after you have a clear idea of what you want. And never forget that it's acceptable to hone your vision as you develop and gain knowledge.

Being present is one of the most crucial components of living with intention. Our thoughts are frequently dispersed among several projects, plans, and anxieties. The now is all we truly have, but it's simple to lose sight of that. We find tranquility and clarity when we give every moment our whole attention, whether it's a discussion, a task at work, or just taking a stroll. You can let joy into your life by focusing on the present moment and letting go of outside distractions and demands.

Mindfulness is a potent discipline that encourages presence. By practicing mindfulness, we can remain rooted in the here and now by observing our thoughts and feelings objectively. A technique that supports intentional living is mindfulness, which can be achieved through deep breathing, meditation, or simply pausing for a little while to reflect on your life. It teaches us to appreciate every moment without being distracted by worry or other people's expectations. Saying no is another aspect of living with intention. The pressure to satisfy others is one of the most significant problems facing the world today. Even when those demands deplete their energy and divert them from their path, many people feel pressured to live up to external expectations. We are encouraged to let go of our demand for approval by the Let Them Principle. Saying no is a way to preserve your time, energy, and tranquility, not to reject others. Respect yourself enough to set boundaries to say yes to what matters—your goals, happiness, and well-being.

Taking action is the next step in living intentionally. You can't have the life you want with just intentions. You have to act with purpose and determination. Divide your objectives into more manageable, smaller activities. Take one step forward every day. The allure of living intentionally is that even the tiniest activity brings you one step closer to your goal. You also gain confidence in your ability to create the life you want with each action.

Cultivating joy is another aspect of living with intention. Joy is something you actively cultivate; it doesn't just happen. It can be discovered in the little things, the straightforward joys, and the choices you make every day to put your happiness first. All too frequently, individuals put off happiness, believing it will arrive when they accomplish specific goals or when their lives become less stressful. Joy, however, is a choice rather than a destination. Consider this question each day: "What can I do today to bring joy into my life?" It could be as simple as letting yourself relax, having a delicious meal, or spending time laughing with friends.

Embracing thankfulness is another aspect of living joyfully. Focusing on what you have rather than what you need changes your perspective. The commonplace becomes spectacular when one is grateful. It serves as a reminder of the wealth in your life. Whether you write it down or just say it out loud, make it a regular routine to show your thankfulness. By focusing on the good, this straightforward exercise can help you change your energy and increase your happiness.

Accepting change is an important aspect of deliberate life. Like life itself, we are always changing. Maintaining outdated routines, convictions, or objectives that no longer benefit us can impede our development. It's crucial to get rid of things that don't fit your future goals. According to the Let Them Principle, we should let go of things that are beyond our control and concentrate on the ones that we can alter. This could entail altering the way we talk to ourselves, our relationships, or our jobs. It's about evolving and adjusting, understanding that every stage of life presents fresh chances for development and happiness. Making self-care a priority is another essential component of intentional living. We frequently become so preoccupied with attending to the needs of others that we neglect our own. However, living consciously entails realizing that you are your greatest asset. Maintaining your vitality and delight requires taking the time to rest, rejuvenate, and feed your body, mind, and spirit. Make time for things that will help you feel refreshed, like working out, reading, taking in the scenery, or just spending time alone.

Journaling is a very effective method for living an intentional life. Journaling keeps you focused on your objectives and enables you to evaluate your feelings, ideas, and development. You can monitor your progress, spot trends, and acknowledge your accomplishments—no matter how minor—by putting your goals and everyday thoughts in writing. Additionally, journaling is a wonderful technique to acknowledge joyful moments throughout the day and to express thanks. It's a means to document your path to a fulfilled and purposeful existence.

Living intentionally gives you the freedom to design the life you desire without being influenced by other forces. You take charge of your life when your actions reflect your principles. Instead of responding to other people's whims, you take control of your experience. No doubt, life will be difficult, but you'll face them with confidence, clarity, and direction.

Purposeful and joyful living is about growth rather than perfection. It's about choosing to focus on the things that give you happiness, freedom, and serenity every single day. Getting rid of noise, tension, and pressure to be someone else is key. You may design a life that is joyful and profoundly meaningful by adopting the Let Them Principle and acting with intention. Never forget that you always have a choice about how you react to situations in life. You can only experience true joy when you live with purpose and a goal.

The key to leading a joyful and purposeful life is consciously selecting what feels right for you, independent of outside influences. The Let Them Principle advises you to let go of the strain of other people's expectations while being loyal to your inner compass. To assist you in living this way every day, consider the following useful activities, illustrations, and journaling prompts:

1. EXERCISE: MORNING INTENTION SETTING

- **Purpose:** Start each day by consciously deciding what you want from it.
- **How:** As soon as you wake up, take five minutes to reflect. Ask yourself: What do I want to achieve today? How do I want to feel at the end of the day? Use the Let Them Principle to help you focus on your desires, not others' demands. Write down your intention for the day.
- **Example:** "Today, I choose to be present in all my interactions and prioritize joy over perfection."

2. EXERCISE: DAILY JOY CHALLENGE

- **Purpose:** Actively bring moments of joy into your day.
- **How:** Set an intention to do one thing that brings you joy every day, no matter how small. This can be something simple like enjoying a cup of coffee, taking a walk, or reading a chapter of your favorite book. The key is to prioritize moments that are just for you, letting go of distractions and other people's demands.
- **Example:** "Today, I will take 10 minutes to sit outside and just breathe in the fresh air without worrying about anything else."

3. EXERCISE: SAYING NO TO NON-ESSENTIAL DEMANDS

- **Purpose:** Protect your time and energy by learning to say no.
- **How:** Each day, identify one thing that doesn't serve your goals or bring you joy. Practice saying no to that request. The Let Them Principle encourages you to let go of the unnecessary, freeing yourself to focus on what truly matters to you.
- **Example:** "I politely declined an invitation to a gathering that I didn't want to attend. I honored my need for rest and personal time."

4. JOURNALING PROMPT: REFLECTING ON INTENTIONS AND JOY

- **Purpose:** Reflect on how your actions align with your intentions.
- **How:** At the end of each day, ask yourself the following questions:
    - How did I live intentionally today?
    - What moments brought me joy, and how can I invite more of that into my life tomorrow?
    - What external noise or pressure did I let go of today, and how did that feel?
- **Example:** "Today, I chose to focus on my work instead of responding to every email immediately. I felt more in control of my time."

5. EXERCISE: GRATITUDE PRACTICE

- **Purpose:** Cultivate an attitude of gratitude to enhance joy.
- **How:** Before bed, list three things you are grateful for that day. They can be big or small. Gratitude helps shift your focus from what's missing to what's abundant in your life. It fosters contentment and joy.
- **Example:** "I'm grateful for the quiet morning walk, a warm conversation with a friend, and the peaceful evening I spent unwinding."

6. JOURNALING PROMPT: LETTING GO OF EXPECTATIONS

- **Purpose:** Release unrealistic expectations placed on you by others.
- **How:** Reflect on a situation where you felt pressured by others' expectations. Write about how it made you feel and how you can release that pressure using the Let Them Principle. Consider how you can align your actions with your own goals instead of external demands.
- **Example:** "I felt pressured to attend an event I didn't want to go to because I didn't want to disappoint anyone. Next time, I'll remember that it's okay to say no and prioritize my peace."

7. EXERCISE: CREATING A JOY LIST

- **Purpose:** Identify activities that bring you joy and intentionally schedule them.

- **How:** Write down a list of activities that make you happy. These could be anything from spending time with loved ones to taking a quiet bath or dancing to your favorite music. Schedule at least one of these activities into your week.
- **Example:** "I added a 30-minute dance break to my calendar every evening to unwind and boost my energy."

8. JOURNALING PROMPT: LIVING WITH CLARITY

- **Purpose:** Ensure your actions align with your long-term vision.
- **How:** Write about your current goals and how the decisions you make today can help you achieve them. Think about the bigger picture and how living intentionally contributes to your growth. Ask yourself how you can stay focused on your true desires while letting go of distractions.
- **Example:** "My goal is to build a successful career while maintaining a healthy work-life balance. Today, I chose to finish my tasks efficiently so I could enjoy the evening with my family."

9. EXERCISE: MINDFUL BREATHING

- **Purpose:** Stay grounded and reduce stress by focusing on your breath.
- **How:** Take five minutes during the day to sit quietly and focus on your breathing. Inhale deeply for a count of four, hold for four, then exhale for four. This simple practice helps center you, making it easier to let go of external pressures and focus on your intentions.
- **Example:** "I took a short break in the middle of my busy workday to practice mindful breathing. I felt more clear-headed and ready to tackle the next task."

10. EXERCISE: VISUALIZING YOUR JOY

- **Purpose:** Envision the life you want to create, filled with intention and joy.
- **How:** Spend a few minutes visualizing your ideal day, one where you are living intentionally and joyfully. Picture yourself engaging in activities that align with your goals and values. Notice the feelings of peace and fulfillment that come from this visualization. Use it as motivation to move forward with intention.
- **Example:** "I visualized waking up to a quiet morning, enjoying a healthy breakfast, and spending time working on my passion project. This inspired me to prioritize those things today."

By incorporating these exercises into your daily routine, you will gradually create a life filled with intention and joy. The Let Them Principle empowers you to stay grounded in your own desires, free from the noise and expectations of others. Remember, living with intention is not about perfection but about progress. It's about actively choosing what feels right for you, letting go of distractions, and embracing the moments that bring you true happiness.

Embracing Endless Possibilities

The Let Them Principle offers a transformative approach to living life on your terms, rooted in the power of letting go of unrealistic expectations and focusing on what matters most. We give ourselves access to a life full of tranquility, meaning, and the chance to follow our genuine desires when we liberate ourselves from the demands of other people and the incessant cacophony of outside influences. This idea is more than simply a framework for thinking; it's a way of life that promotes empowerment and authenticity and has the power to significantly alter the course of our lives. Adopting the Let Them Principle will eventually result in a more contented and grounded life in addition to stress relief.

We become more focused and clearer when we prioritize our needs and values. We create room for what really matters when we break the cycle of striving for approval from others or meeting strict expectations. This type of mental change not only increases our inner tranquility but also improves our relationships, productivity at work, and general life satisfaction. Adopting this approach gives us greater control over our time, energy, and emotions, which leads to a closer relationship with both the outside world and ourselves.

THE LONG-TERM BENEFITS OF LETTING THEM

In the long run, the Let Them Principle is revolutionary. The influence of this theory grows over time by consistently putting the ideas of self-confidence, clarity, and letting go of outside influences into practice. These changes may appear to be minor ones at first, but with repeated practice, they add up to long-lasting advantages that affect every aspect of your life.

A GREATER SENSE OF TRANQUILITY

The sensation of calm that comes with adopting the Let Them Principle is the most obvious advantage. The anxiety of continuously measuring up is released when we let go of the urge to dictate how other people see us or how things "should" go. Setting limits, letting go of other people's expectations, and allowing ourselves to live according to who we are are the keys to this serenity.

In a study on stress and mindfulness, researchers found that participants who practiced mindfulness, which is similar to relinquishing control, experienced a significant reduction in stress and an increase in life satisfaction over time. Focusing on the here and now, letting go of what other people may think, and letting our inner compass guide us is a powerful practice. Our lives become more peaceful the more we let go.

BETTER CONNECTIONS

The Let Them Principle's effect on relationships is another long-term advantage. We can create more genuine connections with our loved ones, friends, and romantic partners when we let go of the impulse to dominate or win their approval. We can share ourselves in a way that is authentic to who we are, and we can accept others as they are instead of looking for approval. Consider the case study of Laura, a lady who worked for years to achieve the professional accomplishment her family expected of her. Laura eventually adopted the Let Them Principle after years of stress and unhappiness. She became more self-centered and started talking candidly with her family about her need for independence and space. Her relationships with her family significantly improved as a result of these discussions, which eventually brought about a greater level of respect and understanding. Enhanced concentration and productivity.

Your productivity automatically rises when you put aside the distractions of other people's opinions and concentrate on your own objectives. You can prioritize activities that help you succeed and learn to say no to things that don't fit with your path by discovering and adhering to your unique beliefs. Increased productivity and a feeling of achievement result from this focus.

Think about John, a businessman who was continuously urged in different ways by people requesting his time, advice, and favors. He was unable to attain the success he had always envisioned until he adopted the Let Them Principle and began establishing boundaries. John grew his firm by concentrating on his own objectives rather than attempting to please everyone around him, thanks to his newly discovered capacity to prioritize what really mattered.

IMPROVED EMOTIONAL HEALTH

We can live truly when we let go of unattainable goals and expectations, free from the emotional weights that other people place on us. As we overcome the need for continual acceptance or the fear of disappointing people, adopting this mindset gradually improves our emotional health.

People who prioritize managing their emotions over repressing or controlling them report improved mental health and increased enjoyment, according to studies on emotional intelligence. According to the Let Them Principle, people should choose not to internalize the emotional baggage of others, embrace their own feelings, and establish emotional boundaries. A more balanced mental state and improved emotional regulation result from this.

HAVING FINANCIAL INDEPENDENCE

Financial independence can also eventually result from letting go of needless outside constraints. You make decisions that benefit your long-term financial well-being when you base them on your actual objectives and values rather than on what society considers success. This could entail spending less on things that don't interest you or devoting time to pursuits that are in line with your goals and passions.

Successful financial coach Anna discovered that she could create long-lasting riches by refocusing her attention from impressing people with material possessions to investing in experiences and financial literacy. She adopted the Let Them Principle after realizing that deliberate acts that were consistent with her basic beliefs, rather than material belongings, were what brought her satisfaction. Her financial circumstances thus significantly improved.

INCREASED SELF-BELIEF

The significant boost in self-confidence that results from having faith in oneself and one's judgment is one of the Let Them Principle's biggest long-term advantages. You start to trust yourself more when you stop looking to other people for approval and start making decisions based on your inner truth. Since trust boosts confidence, it helps you succeed in all areas of life.

According to case studies, people who prioritize their goals and values and can separate them from others' opinions are more likely to succeed and be happy.

Your confidence in your capacity to make choices and overcome obstacles will grow as you continue to adopt this approach.

CASE STUDIES OF REAL-LIFE TRANSFORMATIONS

CASE STUDY 1: MARK'S PATH TO SELF-COMFORT

Despite his success as a lawyer, Mark was always feeling overburdened by the demands of his family, friends, and clients. He had trouble juggling business and personal obligations, always agreeing to requests out of concern that he would let people down if he didn't. Mark started prioritizing time for his personal life, establishing clear boundaries at work, and saying no when needed after embracing the Let Them Principle. He not only found more time for his family throughout the course of the following year, but he also performed better at work. Mark's story demonstrates how letting go of other people's expectations may result in both personal and professional fulfillment.

CASE STUDY 2: SARAH'S REVOLUTIONARY CHANGE

Sarah had always battled body image issues, seeking external affirmation for her appearance and comparing herself to others all the time. She started focusing on her own ideals and letting go of the pressure to live up to social beauty standards after reading about the Let Them Principle. She adopted a self-love perspective and began self-care routines that focused on feeding her body rather than altering it to get favor from others. Sarah's relationship with food and exercise changed from one of restriction to one of empowerment as her confidence increased over time. Her metamorphosis serves as an example of how the Let Them Principle can promote long-term mental health and self-acceptance.

CASE STUDY NO. 3: THE STRENGTH OF RELEASING IN PARTNERSHIPS

In her relationships, Emma had always taken the lead and frequently gave more than she got in return. She felt that she needed to continuously give of herself and attend to the needs of others in order to be loved. She felt worn out and unfulfilled as a result. Emma began prioritizing her own needs and wants and saying no when she felt overburdened after using the Let Them Principle. She gained the ability to speak honestly and frankly with people around her. Her relationships grew stronger over time, and she was surrounded by others who valued her limits and encouraged her to be who she truly was. Emma's story serves as a potent reminder that relationships can become stronger and more satisfying when unreasonable demands are let go.

YOUR JOURNEY TO LASTING PEACE AND CONFIDENCE

Your path to enduring tranquility and self-assurance is a constant process of development rather than a final destination. It's about embracing your flaws, learning to trust yourself, and letting go of the things that are holding you back. As you proceed with implementing the Let Them Principle, keep in mind that every action, no matter how minor, contributes to a greater change in the direction of a fulfilling and true existence. Change is a slow process, but when done consistently and intentionally, it can have profoundly transforming effects.

Consider when you first came across the concept of Letting Them—the idea of establishing boundaries, of letting go of the expectations of others, and of accepting your actual wishes. You probably sensed a glimmer of possibility at that precise moment. However, as you use this notion more thoroughly, you can also experience resistance or periods of uncertainty. Recognize that this is a typical stage of development. The real change occurs when you question your old behaviors and step outside of your comfort zone. As you practice, it becomes easier to shift from limitation to freedom.

The ability to regain your own power is one of the most potent features of the Let Them Principle. It serves as a reminder that you are responsible for your life. You make room for something greater each time you let go of someone or something that no longer serves you. Every act of letting go is an act of self-empowerment, regardless of the source—a limiting mindset, an unpleasant relationship, or the ongoing pressure to live up to others' expectations. This shows you trust yourself enough to prioritize.

As you proceed on this path, reflect on your past accomplishments. Consider how your decisions, behaviors, and thoughts have changed since you initially adopted the Let Them Principle. You now respect your time, know when to say no, and prioritize your own objectives over continuously attempting to meet other people's expectations. Perhaps you're starting to feel more at ease in your day-to-day existence or that your stress levels have dropped. Although these adjustments may appear small at first, they form the foundation of long-term tranquility and self-assurance.

It's important to remember that this path continues into the future. Sometimes the need to please other people or to satisfy demands from outside sources will cause you to revert to your old habits. It's alright. The important thing is to keep on with the procedure. Growth does not occur in a linear fashion. It resembles a spiral in that you occasionally revisit earlier classes, but each time you do, you acquire fresh perspective and advance to a new level of comprehension. Perfection is not necessary for your confidence and tranquility. They result from treating oneself with kindness, accepting where you are at the moment, and persistently working to improve. Recognize that you are a work in progress as you proceed. The wonderful thing about learning is that there is always more to discover. The trip itself is just as worthwhile as the final destination.

Begin each day with a purpose. Establish a clear goal for the day as soon as you get up. What are you hoping to achieve? In what way do you wish to feel? It could be a particular goal you wish to accomplish or something as basic as living in the present. In addition to providing you with focus and direction, setting an intention serves as a reminder that you are in charge of your energy and actions. Take a minute to consider your progress at the end of the day. Honor the victories, no matter how minor, and accept the difficulties without passing judgment.

Additionally, it's critical to constantly assess your surroundings. Do the individuals in your life encourage your personal development? Are you surrounded by people who value your authenticity and respect your boundaries? If not, it could be time to cut ties with those who sap your energy or impede your advancement. Surround yourself with people who push you to your full potential and help you calm and confident.

Mindfulness is another effective technique to use. Be mindful of your thoughts, feelings, and behaviors while remaining in the moment. Take note of when you're beginning to fall back on old routines or when other influences are affecting your choices. Being mindful keeps you centered and in touch with who you really are. Instead of responding to outside forces, it enables you to make decisions based on your principles.

Action is the key to growth, so make a daily commitment to taking tiny, goal-aligned steps. Setting limits, refusing distractions, and scheduling self-care are just a few of the small steps that add up over time and bring about long-lasting change. Never undervalue the influence of routines. Every choice you make to preserve your tranquility and respect your actual self builds up, and one day you'll look back and see how far you've come.

Finally, keep in mind that your path is distinct. There isn't a single, universal route to tranquility and self-assurance. It's okay if what works for someone else doesn't work for you. The Let Them Principle's beauty lies in its ability to provide you the freedom to create a life that is true to your own values and aspirations. If something doesn't fit your vision, change your plan. Trust yourself to make the best choices.

In summary, enduring peace and confidence are processes rather than final goals. Continue applying the Let Them Principle to find that the more you let go of things that no longer serve you, the more room you make for what matters. Your path is one of ongoing development, self-awareness, and metamorphosis. You are entering a life of independence, tranquility, and unwavering confidence by consistently and consciously adopting these values.

I therefore issue a challenge to you: today, take the next step. Consider the lessons you've learned first, and then act on them. What are you prepared to give up today? In the future, how will you prioritize goals and peace? You are empowered to shape the future, and the options are virtually limitless. Have faith in yourself, be dedicated to your personal development, and never forget that you can achieve peace and self-assurance at any time.

Made in the USA
Monee, IL
07 January 2025

76231902R00072